Review Copy

*

Publication Date Sept. 19, 1941

Price $2.50

581620

**MARY AND JOHN GRAY
LIBRARY
LAMAR UNIVERSITY
BEAUMONT, TEXAS**

Gail Borden, Pioneer

Gail Borden, in later life

Gail Borden, Pioneer

by

Clarence R. Wharton

AUTHOR OF

El Presidente (Life of Santa Anna)
History of Texas
San Jacinto, the Sixteenth Decisive Battle
Satanta, Chief of the Kiowas

Illustrations by Warren Hunter

1941

THE NAYLOR COMPANY
PUBLISHERS . . . SAN ANTONIO, TEXAS

Copyright, 1941 by

THE NAYLOR COMPANY

Printed in the United States of America
All rights reserved. This book, or
parts thereof, may not be reproduced
in any form without the permission of
the copyright owner.

To the memory of Henry Lee Borden, grandson of John P. Borden, friend of my earlier days.

PREFACE

Gail Borden was one of the benefactors of the race and linked his name with a great industry which has through more than eighty years grown in importance and volume. Now, sixty-seven years after he passed away, his name is a household word in all the world.

He was a pioneer on two frontiers. He and his three brothers who came into the wilderness with him, more than one hundred years ago, helped win the West and were powerful factors in the great movement which extended our frontiers to the Pacific. After these things had been done, yet in middle life, he turned his talents to the frontiers of science and gave the last half of his life to the exploration of those vast domains in which lie hidden the simple truths whose discovery and development have had and are having today a controlling effect on the destiny of the race.

His life was full of romantic interest and his name and fame will increase with the passing of the years.

—*Clarence R. Wharton*

CONTENTS

		PAGE
GAIL BORDEN		Frontispiece
PREFACE		vii

CHAPTER		PAGE
I	THE BORDENS MIGRATE	1
II	TEXAS	13
III	THE BORDENS DECIDE	25
IV	THE OLD THREE HUNDRED	32
V	THE BORDENS GO TO TEXAS	57
VI	GAIL BORDEN HELPS WRITE THE FIRST TEXAS CONSTITUTION	70
VII	THE BORDENS GO TO WAR	83
VIII	THE BORDENS STILL AT WAR	96
IX	THE BORDENS RETURN HOME	113
X	THE GAIL BORDENS GO TO GALVESTON	136
XI	GAIL BORDEN GOES TO LONDON	159
XII	NEW FRONTIERS	178
XIII	LAST YEARS OF GAIL BOBDEN	201
XIV	GAIL BORDEN'S NAME GOES MARCHING ON	210
BIBLIOGRAPHY		213
INDEX		219

Chapter I

THE BORDENS MIGRATE

On they came, a constant stream of human beings pouring out of New England into the vast West—over the mountains, down the rivers, groups of men, families and groups of families lured to the lands of promise in those vast wild woodlands we now call Ohio, Indiana, Illinois and the still vaster, wilder areas farther west and farther south. Sometimes these units or groups traveled by wagons drawn by horses, or more often oxen, sometimes by sled, or on horseback, and those who could reach their destination by water went the easier way by boat, raft or flat-boat.

These itinerant New Englanders were seeking milder winters, richer lands, seeking adventure, seeking the fulfillment of the promise that lures men into the unknown. The War of 1812 had just closed and there came that brief after the war period when the pent up energies of a nation were turned to the enterprises of peace.

One of these thousands of migratory families came from western New York, Norwich Township, Chenango County, and after endless hardships stranded on the margin of the Ohio River opposite Cincinnati where it stopped for a season in beautiful northern Kentucky. The Gail Bordens were typical Yankee folks with nearly two hundred years of New England ancestry.

The first Gail Borden was born in Rhode Island in 1745 and Gail II was born there in 1777 and there he married Philadelphia Wheeler in 1801. She was a great-granddaughter of the great and good Roger Williams, who is accredited as the founder of the little commonwealth of Rhode Island. The third Gail, their oldest son, was born in Norwich on November 9, 1801, and after him came

The Bordens Migrate

Thomas Henry in 1804, Paschal Pavalo in 1806, and John Petit in 1812.

A hardy, hard-faced man, a meek looking sad-faced woman, and four sturdy, healthy boys ranging from the age of fifteen to a baby of three, tackled the practical problem of finding a livelihood in northern Kentucky. The thrifty father leased land and planted and gathered a single harvest here, then he heard of a better land to the west and was off after that mirage of promise which was leading thousands of New Englanders over the mountains, down the rivers into the dark and bloody West. Three hundred thousand of these restless, nomadic folks had poured into Ohio and more than sixty thousand had pushed on into Indiana before the Bordens came.

The far West then—the Middle West of our day—was a vast forest where a dozen variety of trees grew in luxurious abundance, oak trees that measured twenty feet in circumference and towered one hundred feet. And these dark, dreary forests were filled with every variety of wild life from the panther to the polecat, from the majestic wild turkey to the equally wild pigeon which flew in such swarms that they darkened the sun and broke the branches of the trees in which they rested from their flight.

In the early spring of 1816 the Gail Bordens had gathered their chattel effects, carefully packed away their household goods, which included a well-worn Bible which had come down from the great and good great-grandfather Roger Williams, and were more or less securely housed on a rude raft which was dignified with the name of flat-boat and were off down the Ohio.

After they had followed the meandering course of the crooked river for a week and negotiated big horseshoe bends, they reached a place where the stream seemed to have wearied of winding about and made a twenty mile dash to the due south. The rude flat-boat was nosed into the right bank in the shadow of an everlasting forest at a nameless place in the Territory of Indiana in what afterwards became Jefferson County, and ten miles below a place which afterwards became the town of Madison. Towns, municipalities and counties had a habit in those days of being born Washington, Jefferson and Madison. It was some years before they had taken on the Jackson habit.

Here on a high bank at a place where the view of the broad expanse of the mighty river was sublime, the fugitive New Englanders lighted their campfire. Their chattel effects were laboriously unloaded and a grim-faced father and a sad-faced mother and four sturdy children looked about in awe at the wild western woods.

Although they seemed alone in the solitude of the forest, there were in fact ten thousand other families not vastly different, dragging

The Bordens Migrate

their weary way into the Indiana woods this year.

Down the Ohio, almost at the southernmost tip of the State, in the same year and almost the same month, another fugitive family of New England stock was crossing from Kentucky into the Pigeon Creek country. There was a hard-faced father and a sad-faced mother and two children; the older, a boy of nine, was Abraham Lincoln.

And while the Bordens hewed and hunted and dug for a livelihood up in Jefferson County, the thriftless, shoddy, sorry-looking Tom Lincoln led his sorrowful-looking little family to the Posey farm on Pigeon Creek. The second Gail Borden was a better man than the sloven, slipshod, shiftless second Thomas Lincoln—but this is the story of the Bordens and not the Lincolns.

Life in Indiana one hundred twenty years ago—life anywhere in the western country, in fact life anywhere in the world when its real conditions are known, would seem intolerable to the present generation.

The Bordens had to build a home and find a living off the country while they did so. There was meat in more or less abundance, for a good hunter often got "his limit" of deer in a few hours and "his limit" was all he could carry home. But bread—there was the difficulty. When the corn crop was matured there was grain, but there were few mills and often it was a two days journey to some little grist mill which Dennis Hanks says could not grind corn faster than a hound could eat it. So most of the corn was pulverized on a stone or a stump.

Buckskin breeches and coonskin caps were the vogue. It is said that the first wagon ever driven into Indiana with wheels other than the wooden cross-section of a tree came in 1814. Whiskey was a much more common drink than coffee—and such whiskey! Someone said of it that a drink of it would make a cottontail rabbit tackle a panther. While grist mills were scarce yet there were numerous convenient distilleries which furnished this terrible stuff.

The log houses were small squalid affairs, usually one room for the whole family and the double log house with a hallway between was an edifice of elegance. A traveler who went through the Indiana woods during these years and wrote of his travels, told that typical of the habitations was a single log room which served as kitchen, living-room, bedroom and dining-room where the meals were served in a hand-basin, often without knives and forks; that such an abode frequently housed ten persons.

Along with the pioneers came the itinerant preacher and the itinerant pedagogue who had to operate without churches or school houses. Often the precocious boy who had learned to

The Bordens Migrate

read and write, perhaps taught by his mother, would teach a school when he was old enough to keep some show of discipline, and before Gail Borden III was twenty he had taught two terms of school in their settlement.

The best openings for young men who wanted to take up professional careers were the bar and surveying. Hundreds of young men who could not maintain themselves in the sixth grade of a modern school, read the statutes and a few law books they could not understand and got licenses to practice law and went into politics.

Surveyors were made almost as easily. There were millions of acres of land to be surveyed in every state and territory. A young man who mastered some rudiments of mathematics soon learned to make the calculations necessary to measure land and his services were in demand everywhere. Both Gail, Jr. and his next brother, Thomas Henry, three years his junior, learned land surveying well before they were twenty-one.

Gail, Sr., had acquired the skill of a tanner and varied his hunting and farming with the dressing of hides. Paschal Pavalo, the third son, acquired the technique of blacksmithing.

The Borden boys grew up rapidly, as boys do even now, and five and a half years in the Indiana woods found Gail, Jr., in his twenty-first year, tall, slender, with a tendency to stoop and a cough which was aggrevated by the long, hard winters. Thomas Henry, eighteen, was a powerful fellow with no limit to his physical prowess and endurance.

The problem of the ages was up for discussion in the Borden household—what would the boys do, where would they go? That they must go somewhere seemed obvious. That Gail needed to go to a milder climate was agreed, and that Thomas Henry would go into a more energetic environment was conceded. During all the years they had lived on the banks of the Ohio they had seen constant streams of people going down the great river to the far south, down to the Louisiana lands and to the Spanish countries beyond, and strange stories came up from these half-fabled lands—lands of plantations where sugar and cotton were raised by slave labor and roses bloomed the year round.

A few steamboats were now plying on the river and passage to and from New Orleans had become much simpler. But the flat-boat was still much in vogue and folks all the way from Cincinnati would send produce down the Ohio to the Mississippi and down the Mississippi to New Orleans where it could be taken by real boats to Gulf and Atlantic ports. Gail and Thomas Henry planned a journey to the southern country where the older brother hoped to improve his cough and Thomas his fortunes. They found persons at Madison and other near-

The Bordens Migrate

by places who planned sending a flat-boat cargo down the river and were willing to entrust its carriage and disposal to the Borden boys.

The flat-boat, a kind of dignified raft, had long been a familiar means of downstream river navigation, but presented unsurmountable difficulties for the return trip. They were often made of the trunks of huge poplar trees lashed together, sometimes sixty feet long. On them the voyagers placed cargoes of meat, corn, flour, hides, tobacco and whatever the westerners could sell at New Orleans where for nearly a century boats from many nations had come for cargoes. While the steamboat had now been on the river for nearly ten years it had not yet displaced the primitive navigation, and all the way from Cincinnati farmers, merchants and traders braved the long voyage to the New Orleans market. Sometimes a whole community would combine in building one of these floating monsters and freighting it with an assorted cargo of hides and hams, wheat, corn, tobacco and whiskey. Immigrants who were on their way to the South often found passage as a kind of super cargo. Sometimes they would go down in fleets, ganged together for mutual protection against robbers and river mishaps.

They usually left the Ohio in early spring to get the aid of the strong current of the swollen rivers, but waterways were open the year round. It took from two to four weeks to go from Louisville to New Orleans, but coming back was a venture which would have taxed Ulysses. To come back with the average poplar log flat-boat was out of the question and often the traders came back in rowboats which required sometimes one hundred days from New Orleans to St. Louis.

Chambers in his *Mississippi Valley,* says that in going upstream the boatman suffered from the many bends he had to negotiate and would often have to detour fifty miles to make a progress of five; that to avoid the centrifugal sweep of the current he had to take the inside curve and since the course of the stream was sinuous and the curves frequent, there were endless crossings and recrossings from shore to shore to keep the inside and at each crossing the boatman would be carried downstream a mile by the midstream current.

Early in the century before the return trip could be made by steamboat, traders from the Ohio often took their cargoes down in three weeks, sold out at New Orleans and took a boat for Baltimore and came home four months later by the upper Ohio.

But the Borden boys were not seriously worried about getting back home. In the first place they had little notion of coming back and in the second place they could get steamboat passage if such a necessity arose.

It was a new world into which the Borden

The Bordens Migrate

boys were going when they swung their raft into the Ohio current in the late midsummer and saw the figures of the watchers fade and the outline of the homestead grow dim. Father, mother and the two younger boys stood long on the bluff and watched the clumsy boat recede into the dim horizon down the deep Ohio. Sunset and twilight came and after that the dark and the youthful voyagers drifted away in the night to an unknown future in unknown lands. Long years full of stirring events on far-flung frontiers were to pass before they were to again see the Indiana woods.

As the boat passed down into the lower Mississippi they saw the vast forests hung with bearded moss and the plantations of cotton, sugar and indigo, and here and there gleaming through the trees the outlines of a plantation mansion more splendid than anything they had ever beheld. They had often talked with river voyagers who had been down to Louisiana and Mississippi and had brought back fairy tales of the plantation lands where lordly planters were served by numberless slaves, planters whose wealth was boundless and whose daughters were beautiful, and now as they drifted along into Dixie the visions and dreams that have filled the minds of adventurous youth in all the ages beckoned them on. They had heard of Louisiana and Mississippi from men who had been there and they had heard of the vast half-mythical land called Texas, but not from men who had been there, for men who had ventured into Texas had not often returned.

New Orleans was all excitement when the Borden boys landed with their cargo of Indiana produce, but not over the incident of their coming for flocks and fleets of such boats had been coming down since Oliver Pollock of Baltimore had headed the first river raft of such merchandise to the landing in the days of Count O'Reilly seventy years before. The excitement was the news from Texas which it was hard for men to believe. Stephen F. Austin, the first and the great Empresario, had just arrived on a steamboat coming from Natchitoches and was at the Richardson House and was confirming the rumors that he had a concession from the authorities down in Mexico to convoy three hundred Louisiana families into forbidden Texas and found a colony beyond the borders which for one hundred years had been closed to all comers and guarded by Spanish soldiers.

Chapter II

TEXAS

The vast country lying west of the Sabine, west of the borders of Louisiana, and stretching far towards the Californias, had for centuries been a closed, mysterious land whose borders were supposed to be guarded by Spanish troops ready to deal death to all intruders. More than one hundred years before there had been a controversy about its ownership between France and Spain, and Spanish soldiers and priests had come with the sword and the crucifix and made a feeble gesture toward occupying it. The French had established a trading post on Red River at Natchitoches, which they claimed was well within Louisiana, and the Spaniards squatted on the little Arroyo Hondo ten miles away and built a squalid little presidio and mission which festered in obscurity for fifty years, but which told the world in general and the French in particular that this was the easternmost limits of their Texas.

Then came the French and Indian War and when England was about to take all of the French possessions in North America the French one fine day in 1765 ceded Louisiana to Spain to keep it out of England's hands. There were now no borders to guard between Louisiana and Texas; the Spaniards moved into Louisiana, and Count O'Reilly, the Spanish Governor, to prove the presence of Spanish sovereignty hung a dozen or more of the most prominent French citizens of New Orleans, after which this sovereignty was generally recognized along the Mississippi and far to the west to the Californias.

In the last days of the century the Spanish monarch, Charles IV, wanted a kingdom for his nephew who was his son-in-law, the Duke of Parma, and Napoleon I, who had gathered up an assortment of small kingdoms here and there,

Texas

traded King Charles the Italian province of Etruria for Louisiana, and on October 1, 1800, that vast country which reached from the mouth of the Mississippi north and west to God knows where, became a French province once more.

Then two years later came the sale of the province to the United States who took it with its boundaries unsettled and was quick to claim everything to the setting sun, including Texas. The treaty of San Ildefonso by which this land trade was made, was a secret covenant and for the time being it was kept from the world at large and from the people of Louisiana who had become Spanish after the severe lesson of Count O'Reilly.

In 1801 an American named Philip Nolan, with a dozen venturesome fellows he had picked up in the States and with the permission of the Spanish Governor of Louisiana, came over into Texas to hunt wild horses. When his presence was learned by the Spanish Governor of Texas, soldiers were sent and Nolan was killed and ten of his companions were taken and marched down into Chihuahua where they were charged with the awful offense of having been found in Texas. They were tried in the Spanish court in Chihuahua, but their offense was such a heinous one that the record was sent all the way across the ocean in order that the King might pass judgment, all the while the culprits remaining in dungeons.

Now the King in those days was ruled by his wicked wife who was ruled by a sorry fellow named Godoy. In due time the weak King, or the wicked Queen, or the sorry Godoy, or whoever had the final say about Nolan's men, got around to the case. One day in February, 1807, a royal decree was written that one out of five of these fellows should be hanged and the other eight kept at very hard labor for ten years. This decree came all the way back to Chihuahua for observance, but one of the culprits had died and one out of each five could not be hanged, so the local authorities decided after much deliberation that the dignity of the Crown would be conserved by hanging one and putting the other eight at ten years hard labor.

In order to demonstrate the utter impartiality of Spanish justice the Adjutant Inspector had the prisoners brought before the bar and all of them blindfolded. A glass with two dice was placed on a drumhead before them and one by one they threw—the man making the lowest score to be hanged by the neck until he was dead. Ephraim Blackburn, who had come from Kentucky and who threw three and one, was hanged on the spot and the others began their ten years on November 9, 1807.

The details of all this were widely published in the United States from whence these men had come, and it was generally known to all men that the Spanish government would not

Texas

permit intrusions into Texas. This severe warning seemed necessary for now (1807) the United States had taken over Louisiana and was the border neighbor of Texas, and intrusions by these land-hungry folks from the States were much feared by the Spanish authorities in Mexico.

When the United States moved into Louisiana after the purchase, Spain and all Spanish America were full of grave fears and suspicions that these Yankees would come on across the border and gobble up Texas, and a Spanish garrison was stationed at Nacogdoches and troops were on the Sabine to prevent this disaster. For fifteen years these governments glared at each other across the border which had never been defined.

A few years after the execution of the sentence against Nolan's men, which included the execution of Ephraim Blackburn of Kentucky, there was a war for independence going on in Mexico—that country striving to throw off its allegiance to Spain, and all through the Southern States there was much sympathy for the patriot cause from people who wanted an excuse to go into Texas.

An ambitious military expedition was outfitted on the border led by a Lieutenant lately out of West Point who hurried to espouse for Mexico and Texas the cause of independence. The Republican army, as it was called by its leaders, was called Filibusters by the Spanish authorities, a sorry name for zealous advocates for liberty. Nor did these Spanish authorities stop at calling the invaders ugly names. They were lured into a battle on the Medina River beyond San Antonio and literally cut to pieces. A few of the fragments got back across the border with the tale of disaster. From this it was seen that the Spaniards who ruled Mexico, were of the same opinion in 1813 as they were in 1807 when Nolan's men were disposed of. They did not want emigration from the States. The fate of the Filibusters added to that of Nolan's men well convinced all people in the United States who were interested in the subject that it was unwise and unsafe to venture across the border.

All the while Spain and the United States were trying to fix the boundaries and the Spaniards were cautious to make no admission that their claim to Texas was not bona fide.

After a long time and slow negotiations, his Catholic Majesty, as the King of Spain was called, and the United States, made a boundary treaty agreeing on the limits between the Louisiana purchase and the Spanish possessions in North America known as the Adams de Onis treaty. By its terms the "high contracting parties" agreed that a line beginning at the mouth of the Sabine and following various calls for course and distance to the 42nd parallel on the

Texas

Pacific Ocean should mark the boundary between the two nations. Everybody seemed to think this settled it and Texas was to remain a Spanish country forever. At least the Spaniards thought so and they took a breathing spell and relaxed their exclusion policy for a time with disastrous results as we shall see.

Although it had been more or less Spanish for two hundred years, the only evidence of the fact was three small towns, Nacogdoches, San Antonio, and Goliad and a dozen abandoned Spanish missions here and there. Texas in 1820 was as wild as it was in 1687 when LaSalle first saw its shores. But the boundaries were now fixed, solemnly agreed on, and there was little danger that the Yankees would not understand this. So when in December, 1820, Moses Austin coming from the States and originally from Connecticut, sought permission to bring a Colony of homeseeking settlers from Louisiana into Texas, his petition was received and on January 17, 1821, was granted by the Commandant of the Eastern Internal Provinces of New Spain down at Monterrey.

When Moses Austin died the following June and his son Stephen took up his enterprise, he was received with cordial esteem by Antonio Martinez, the Spanish Governor of Texas at San Antonio, and told to go out into a virgin land along the coast, larger than the New England States, and select a site for his Colony of three hundred homeseekers to be brought from Louisiana. He and the Governor agreed on the land bounties which were to be made to these homeseekers and Austin hurried back to the States to drum up his Colonists. He was now in New Orleans with this news, confirming rumors that had been rife all during the summer, and this was the biggest news item of the year in old New Orleans.

Austin issued an advertisement which soon appeared in many of the little four page Southern papers telling of his grant and inviting homeseekers to join him in his enterprise. The Spanish authorities, he told, had agreed to a bounty of a section of 640 acres of land to each single man, two sections to a family and under special conditions as much as three sections.

All this brought on Texas talk in every barroom, on every street corner and everywhere in New Orleans that people foregathered. Old-timers who remembered the fate of Nolan's men and had seen the surviving Filibusters when they got back to tell their tale, were incredulous and slow to believe that three hundred families from Louisiana or anywhere else in the States would be permitted in Texas.

The papers published little paragraphs of Texas news, some of them that the venture of Moses Austin had fallen down; another that it had been confirmed and two hundred families were on the way.

Texas

Tall tales from Texas were told everywhere and survivors of former ventures which had taken them there were much in evidence with their superior experience.

A New Orleans paper published a story from a traveler, who had been in Texas, about an animal he had seen standing with its chin on a rock and its tail wrapped about a tree some distance away. A group of mustangs came down to drink at a spring nearby, so the story ran, when the beast unwrapped its tail from the tree and threw it around the neck of the largest horse and at the same time grabbed hold of another tree with its forefeet, holding fast while it choked the horse to death with its tail. It then devoured the horse at one meal and departed. The traveler ventured down after the beast was well gone and measured the distance between the rock on which it had its chin and the tree about which it had wound its tail and found it to be fifty-three feet. The animal, so the traveler said, was a rusty color with a head very much like an alligator. When it went away it folded its tail over its back. The traveler proffered to get the affidavits of Pedro Diros and three other witnesses if anyone should doubt his story.

Other travelers who had been in Texas told of the herds of cattle which had descended from those brought by the priests a hundred years before, thousands and thousands wanting only an owner to claim and mark and brand them. Others told of the vast herds of splendid wild horses—thousands and thousands of them galloping over flower-decked prairies, wanting only an owner to lariat and ride them. Others told of the herds of buffalo which came down from the great northwest each autumn all the way to the margin of the sea, thousands and thousands of them with no hunter but the red man to molest them. All who talked told of the millions of acres of lands fit for homesteads.

The Borden boys heard all this and much more during their stay in New Orleans and the Texas fever seized upon them. Having attended to the sale of their cargo they went around daily to the Richardson House where Austin and a coterie of his companions on his late journey to Texas were staying, and sought an interview with the young Empresario. There Austin and Gail Borden stood face to face and each looked into a manly countenance and they formed a friendship that only ended when Borden, pale with grief, stood by Austin's grave on a December day fifteen years later.

Stephen F. Austin—the very name has become synonymous with high honor and manly achievement, was then twenty-seven years old, medium height, slender, almost frail, with large hazel eyes and heavy black hair which hung in a cluster over his fine forehead—a frontiersman born and bred but with a refinement of nature and demeanor which would have been rare in a French nobleman. He spoke with measured caution in a low firm voice and looked directly at his listener in a way to hold his attention and bring conviction.

Yes, he still wanted recruits for his enterprise, young men, family men, men who wanted homes. But when he understood that Gail had come south partly on account of his health, that he had a cough which bordered on lung trouble, he doubted the wisdom of his braving the hardships just now. But when he looked at the athletic, hardy Thomas H. Borden, he thought that Texas needed such men and that it afforded the opportunities for which Thomas sought.

There were around Austin daily a kind of Cabinet of enterprisers who were talking up his plans. There was William Little, the Pennsylvanian who had been with him in Missouri and had ridden with him on his recent journey to Texas and was now about to return with the three hundred. A big loud talking man of forty-five from Georgia named Jesse Thompson was there every day filling himself with enthusiasm and announcing to all concerned, and many who were not, that he was going to be among the first.

Two brothers named Ingram, both surveyors, were anxious to know what Austin thought their chance of profitable employment and he told Seth and Ira Ingram that surveyors would be needed in Texas, and the Borden boys heard this.

Jared E. Groce, a wealthy planter from Mobile, was there and announced his intention to be in Texas with his one hundred Negroes before Christmas.

While they were still considering their course of conduct a chance meeting at the Richardson House threw young Gail Borden with Dr. William Lattimore, a splendid looking, kindly man of forty-five who lived in southern Mississippi about one hundred miles from New Orleans. The Doctor who had long been prominent in the public affairs of Mississippi had called to see Austin and learn more about the Texas venture. He had come from Virginia twenty-five years before, and the stories of Texas had made an impression on his imagination. He seriously contemplated exchanging his Mississippi home for one in the far west. Dr. Lattimore was impressed with the mild mannered, genteel, delicate looking Gail Borden and invited him to come to southern Mississippi where he would find climate suitable to his need and employment as a surveyor.

Chapter III

THE BORDENS DECIDE

Gail and Thomas H. Borden sat on the bank of the dark rolling Mississippi that night and talked long and seriously of the near future before them. Thomas Henry would go to Texas. His mind was made up, and Gail wanted to go with him. When the moon had risen and cast a yellow light over the great river, they trudged back over a muddy path to their lodging house.

Their verdict was made up. Thomas Henry would take a steamer for the Ohio River country at once and would settle up the accounts for the merchandise they had brought down, would attend to some other unfinished petty business, including the parental assent, and would join the three hundred and Texas. Gail would go up to southern Mississippi for the winter and as soon as his cough subsided and his strength seemed ample for such a hardy venture, he would join his brother in Texas.

In the latter days of November the Borden brothers watched the schooner "Lively," the Texas Mayflower, depart with its cargo to Texas and immediately afterwards Tom took passage on a river steamer to their home in Indiana while Gail went to Mississippi with his new friend.

Southwest Mississippi one hundred twenty years ago was part of what we call the Old South, the Deep South—although it was a new or pioneer country. A New Englander who migrated to the Ohio-Indiana woods remained a Yankee. He was a bit more primitive in his wild western environment, but he retained most of the notions of his ancestors. But one who went away down South went into a different atmosphere, a different world. Long ago the South had developed the great cotton industry and had at least one cash crop which was cultivated chiefly by slaves. The people down South had

The Bordens Decide

also developed an indigo industry and sugar fields which together with their other products common to the States just north, brought more wealth to the South than to the other States. With this wealth sprang, as always, a kind of self-styled aristocracy, who with some leisure developed an intellectual atmosphere which made for culture. A people who had to spend all their waking hours working for a living had little time for intellectual pursuits and this was the fortune of the newcomers in the Indiana woods. They had not yet developed the great corn and wheat production and markets which in a later generation enabled them to outstrip the South when it fell under the blow of the Civil War.

New Orleans was founded in 1718 and had been a great trade center, market and port for over one hundred years before Chicago was begun. But the rich production of the grain belts did not materialize and produce an aristocracy until after the war when the South fell under the curse of defeat which retarded its growth for fifty years.

The New Englander who came to Mississippi or Alabama one hundred twenty years ago soon became an enthusiast of the "peculiar institution of the South," and thousands of them came. Environment made all the difference. Thomas Lincoln and Samuel Davis both lived in western Kentucky in 1808 and 1809, not more than one hundred miles apart, and were men of much the same type—both from Pennsylvania stock, although the Lincolns had come originally from New England. Always moving about, the Lincolns and the Davises had for a hundred years lived here and there in Pennsylvania, Virginia, the Carolinas and Georgia and here in the early years of the century they were near the borderland between North and South where Jefferson Davis was born in June, 1808, and Abraham Lincoln the following February.

Samuel Davis, who had moved his family from State to State for years and was now the father of ten children, moved again, this time to southwest Mississippi. He left Kentucky for the cotton country and went to work with his children in the cotton fields. An older son, Joseph, soon became a successful and wealthy planter and was able to give his younger brother Jefferson a plantation. Taken from the cotton field to college and then the owner of a plantation and slaves, Jefferson Davis was an aristocrat. Years later, speaking from the floor of the United States Senate in defense of slavery, he said that the South had solved the problem of human relations and industrial happiness; that an intelligent white man need not labor there, but could have this menial employment done by slave labor. He told his colleagues in the Senate and the listening world that slavery

The Bordens Decide

in the South had superseded the necessity for an order of nobility.

A very few years after the migration of Samuel Davis and his prolific family to the Deep South, Thomas Lincoln's little family, including the seven-year-old boy Abe, trekked out of Hardin County, Kentucky, across Ohio into the Indiana woods, the same year the Bordens came down the Ohio to Jefferson County, Indiana. Who can say that if Samuel Davis had taken his son into these forest solitudes and he had grown up in Indiana and Illinois that he might not have been the great emancipator, and that if Thomas Lincoln had moved down into southwest Mississippi and Abraham had grown up on a Southern plantation that he might not have been the President of the Southern Confederacy.

Gail Borden, Jr. with nearly two centuries of New England background and a boyhood in the Indiana forest, was now in the Deep South. Here in Amite County, Mississippi, he saw trees taller than the oak and sycamore on the Ohio and he saw pioneer cabins as squalid and families as poor as the Indiana backwoodsmen. But he saw something else here. There were here and there large plantations whose owners lived in a style entirely unknown in New England or Indiana. Perhaps the plantations and the Negroes who tilled them were mortgaged, often hypothecated by ambitious proprietors for money with which to buy more lands and more Negroes, but there were more commodious homes and what was much more important, there were libraries.

Dr. William Lattimore had come into the Mississippi wilderness twenty years before and located in Wilkinson County near Natchez, the very county to which Samuel Davis had moved when he came wandering from Kentucky. Dr. Lattimore had been instrumental in having Amite County carved out of Wilkinson and lived on an ample plantation ten miles south of the county seat town of Liberty, a plantation which he had given the poetic name of Green Valley. Little Liberty, which to this day has never had a population in excess of one thousand, was a community of planter folks, who through more than a century have been genteel, cultured, kindly and highly hospitable. The little red brick courthouse which Gail Borden saw there in 1822 still stands, perhaps the oldest in Mississippi.

The tall slender lad with a bad cough was welcomed and was soon at home among these genial people. There was surveying to be done and he unpacked his transit and Jacob's staff. He read books from Dr. Lattimore's library and now and then taught a rural school. Here in these quiet congenial surroundings he was to spend nearly seven years.

Two days before Gail Borden left with Dr.

The Bordens Decide

Lattimore for southwest Mississippi, Thomas H. Borden had taken a boat for the Ohio expecting to be back in New Orleans in time to join Austin's first contingent of emigrants to Texas which was being hurriedly recruited.

When he reached home with the word of his contemplated migration to wild, mysterious Texas about which only the worst stories of Spanish cruelty had been long related to the folks on the Ohio, there was much debate in the Borden household and serious opposition to his going. But Thomas Henry had seen the world now, had mixed and mingled with those adventurous spirits down in New Orleans who had been in Texas and who were on their way there again, and although only eighteen he was not to be put down by parental objections and on the first day of the New Year he was back in New Orleans on his way to Texas. But Austin and his first Colonists had gone, and Thomas Henry made haste to follow up and join the Old Three Hundred.

Chapter IV

THE OLD THREE HUNDRED

Although Thomas H. Borden did not arrive with the first installment, he was one of the Old Three Hundred as Austin's first Colonists were called. Austin's first grant, made his father and confirmed in him, authorized the induction of three hundred families from Louisiana. Afterwards he procured four other concessions, but

The Old Three Hundred

a distinction was always claimed by the first comers—The Old Three Hundred.

The first contingents of these Colonists left Louisiana in the late autumn of 1822, one coming overland by way of the Old Spanish Trail, the other on the schooner "Lively" which came around from New Orleans by sea. There were a number of Colonists who came individually and in small groups apart from these two. Probably fewer than one hundred all told started in these autumn expeditions.

The schooner "Lively" in addition to twelve or fifteen immigrants brought supplies and implements that would be needed by the first Colonists and left New Orleans late in November. Austin, after seeing it sail, came up the Mississippi and Red River to Natchitoches and joined the overland immigrants. These overland immigrants reached the Brazos about one hundred fifty miles from its mouth on the last day of the year and founded what has always been called the New Year's Creek Colony.

The schooner "Lively" reached the mouth of the Brazos late in December and most of the immigrants disembarked and started up the river to meet Austin whom they fancied would be coming down to meet them. There was probably a dozen of these immigrants thus left on foot at the mouth of a river whose name they did not even know in a land as primitive as Columbus found three centuries before. The nearest habitation was at San Antonio two hundred miles away. They made their way in row boats and on foot, living off the country as they went.

About sixty miles from the mouth of the river they encountered a great bend where at some remote age in the past when the river was being formed, titanic waves of some prehistoric ocean had cast a great sand-bar, and the river turned its course around it, making a horseshoe bend probably ten miles around with no more than a mile across at the neck of the bend. The sand-bar which formed the interior of this bend was somewhat higher ground than the country round about. At one place in the great curve there were some falls in the river, three or four feet high, which made it impossible to carry a boat upward.

Here these footsore immigrants seeing and hearing nothing of Austin, decided to stop and make a temporary habitation until they could get word from him. Just below the mouth of the bend at a place where the prairie came down on the west of the margin of the river, they set to work to build a log cabin which they finished after a couple of months and it was used as kind of habitation for all of them—kind of a clubhouse, if you please and, by some stretch of the imagination it was called a fort, and since there was a great bend nearby it got the name of Fort Bend.

The Old Three Hundred

Among these first immigrants were William Little who had been in Texas during the preceding summer with Austin, James Beard, William Morton, and his sons and daughters who had come from Alabama, David Fitzgerald, whose names are written forever on the land maps of Texas which will bear them until the end of time. They, of course, could do nothing until they got in contact with Austin who would have to show them where their land would be located.

They liked the country about the Big Bend and when the soft winter sunshine of an open January gilded the land they thought they had found eternal summer. Hearing nothing from Austin they decided to tarry there until he found them.

There was much discussion in the little clubhouse as to where each Colonist would locate his section or his two sections of land and from day to day they tramped over the landscape hunting deer and turkey and looking for home sites. William Morton had a family and daughters and by common consent he was given first choice. He found a great cane-brake, miles on miles of wild cane twenty feet high and as thick as the grass on the prairies which stretched from the east bank of the Brazos for ten miles and here in its margin he built a thatch hut, burned off a few acres of the cane and in the rich fallow ground planted corn from a pouch of seed he had brought with him.

All the while they waited for Austin. Some of the party grew weary and left for the coast hoping to find a boat and passage back to Louisiana while other stragglers came to join them. Among the arrivals in June were Thomas H. Borden and a young man named Walker, who had joined him in New Orleans. They had manned a small boat and with two others had rowed all the way from the mouth of the Mississippi to Galveston Bay. Two of them had taken the boat on down the coast while Borden and Walker had followed footsteps and signs of the first comers to their camp at the big bend.

Only those who have seen the glory of southern Texas in June can visualize the prospect which lured them as they lived beneath the open skies which arched this virgin land.

They joined the long vigil for Austin, who was now six months overdue. Then came word that he had been compelled to go down to the City of Mexico, that there was some trouble about his grant, that it might not be confirmed, that after all they might be driven out or share the fate of Nolan's men, and more of them went away. But Thomas H. Borden stayed on. He had found the land of his dreams—and there was ample time for dreams as the summer season bloomed in its tropical fullness.

Shortly after Austin's arrival on the Brazos

The Old Three Hundred

one hundred miles above, he concluded that it would be well for him to report to Governor Martinez at San Antonio, whom he had not seen since he was there in the preceding July, advising that he had come with his first installment of immigrants and for further instructions as to their location and details as to their land titles.

When he reached San Antonio for that purpose the Governor was very much troubled. The grant to Moses Austin the preceding January had been made by the Spanish Commandant at Monterrey. The Spanish sovereignty had been overthrown in the interim and a new government had been instituted in the City of Mexico. Governor Martinez did not know his status, whether he was to be retained by the new government, nor did he know the status of the land grant that had been made by the fallen sovereignty. And above all he did not know whether a new government would recognize the arrangement he had made with Austin as to the number of Colonists and the amount of land to be awarded them. He expressed these doubts and fears to Austin and suggested that he go at once to the City of Mexico and present his case to the new government.

This was more than the Empresario had bargained for. He did not speak the Spanish language, he was ill-equipped with funds for such a journey and Mexico and the country between was in a wild turbulent state. But seeing that this was necessary, he did not hesitate and named his old friend, James H. Bell, who had come with the first Colonists, to look after them in his absence, and on short notice left for the City of Mexico a thousand miles away.

He rode on horseback to Monterrey where he was advised that it was dangerous to travel on the highway to the City of Mexico and he and a companion disguised themselves as beggars and walked most of the way to the City which he reached the following April.

The advent of this ragged, disguised pedestrian into the foreign City of Mexico in April was not frought with circumstances calculated to make any great impression as to the importance of his coming or the weight of his mission.

Mexico had been a Spanish Province for more than three hundred years, but during the last ten years preceding this event there had been a revolution going on with varying fortunes in which the people of Mexico sought independence from Spain.

In 1821, owing to the defection of Colonel Iturbide who had been the leader of the King's troops, the revolution was brought to a successful termination and the last of the viceroys was constrained to agree with Colonel Iturbide that Mexico should be independent. This was accomplished under what was called the Plan of

The Old Three Hundred

Igula which Iturbide had widely advertised in his last campaign, which guaranteed to the people of Mexico a constitutional monarchy. This Plan of Igula which promised a constitutional monarchy provided that the then King of Spain could come over and become Emperor of Mexico if he so desired, and if he did not so desire he might send his son or any idle Bourbon Prince he might have available. Though several months had elapsed since this kindly offer was made neither the King nor any Bourbon Prince had showed up to claim the throne and Colonel Iturbide could not afford to see a crown and the throne go by default, so he contrived to have himself made Emperor of Mexico. About the time that Austin came walking into the City from the north, Iturbide was being crowned with great pomp and ceremony.

The new Emperor had a Congress, and Austin in time found his way around and presented his petition for a recognition of his father's grants to the proper committee of the new Congress. Although he spoke the language very poorly and was at great disadvantage in many ways, yet his personal appearance after he had taken a bath and shaved and changed raiment; and his mannerisms made a good impression upon these Mexicans and he was accorded a kindly hearing and much consideration. When they understood the nature of his mission and had his assurance he was going to bring good

Catholic families from Louisiana into Texas to cultivate the wilderness, there was little opposition to his plan. But when they came to examine the details of the agreement between him and Governor Martinez by which each single man was to have 640 acres of land, an English section, and each family two English sections, they rebelled. These Spanish gentlemen would not measure their land in English sections. It was suggested that instead of a section that each settler have a labor. Austin asked how much land was in a labor and was told that it was 177 acres, the area which was thought to be suitable for an agriculturist. He was very much perturbed by this and explained to them that he had advertised his plan throughout Louisiana and that his Colonists who had come with him to Texas, as well as those who were on their way, were expecting to get one section and two sections, and that if they were reduced to this labor that he would be regarded as an impostor and the enterprise would be ruined. They felt sorry for him but could not for one moment concede that Mexican or Spanish land could be measured by English sections. Finally out of compassion for him some member of the committee suggested that in addition to the labor they might give his Colonists, who chose to be herdsmen as well as farmers, an adjacent league. Austin asked how much land was in a league and was told that a Spanish league was

The Old Three Hundred

4428 acres. So he compromised the situation with them and instead of one section for a single man and two sections for a married man, it was agreed that every head of a family coming into Texas in his Colony should have a league and a labor and a single man a half league. If the Colonist expected to do cattle raising on a large scale he might have more than one league. These details generously provided for, the Congress was about to finally confirm his grant when a revolution broke out against the new empire. The Emperor promptly suppressed it by dismissing Congress and summoning a committee to govern in its stead. Austin was compelled to re-present his petition to this committee and finally after explaining it all over again he got the approval of the Emperor's committee and was about to depart for home well satisfied with his accomplishments. But before he could get out of town another revolution broke out and the Emperor fled in the night. The first Congress which the Emperor had dissolved a few months before, now reassembled and assumed to rule the country, and Austin was compelled to go before it again. One of its first acts was to disavow everything that the Emperor and his committee had done in the interim and this disavowment destroyed the approval of Austin's grant by the Emperor's committee. But the first Congress in its second session was readily persuaded to confirm what had almost been done by it in the first session and after nearly a year of waiting Austin's grant was finally approved and he was off for home. While the year in Mexico seemed a long tedious one for Austin, it seemed interminable for his Colonists waiting and watching for his return.

No one knew where to go or what to do until he could get some word from Austin. They expected him back in August but August came and went and no news from him and all through the late summer and autumn they watched for his return, and then the winter of 1822 began. They did not dare to build permanent habitations for they did not know whether they would be awarded the land upon which they constructed them. So everywhere on the Brazos and Colorado the Colonists lived in the most primitive fashion, sometimes without even tents; without bread until a corn crop could be raised, they lived entirely on meat. When they could not find deer or buffalo they satisfied themselves with horse-meat from the abundant herds of mustangs that could be approached at least within rifle shot.

The wild beauty of the country appealed to Thomas H. Borden and his young companion. Along the rivers there were deep woodlands, forests of trees unknown to them before, the prairies were covered with flowers, strange kinds that they had never seen. In the early spring there were literally miles of bluebonnets

The Old Three Hundred

which covered the landscape as far as the eye could see; there were other miles of the variegated phlox and the whole country between the Colorado and the Brazos over which these first Colonists were roaming was like a vast woven carpet of beautiful colors.

But this splendid scenery palled on the little handful of newcomers living out of doors on a meat diet, wondering where their homes would be and wondering when Austin would come back from his long stay in Mexico.

Thomas H. Borden very much preferred the country in and around the great bend of the Brazos and thought he would select his section of land there, but Morton and Little, who were there first, expressed a preference for this neighborhood. He and Walker were now joined by Johnson and the three of them started out to find the fairest spot in all the land before them.

Living a life almost as wild as that of the animals around them, they managed to exist through the winter of 1822, thinking that surely with the dawn of the new year Austin would be back. But the winter passed, spring came and yet no tidings of him. Others tired and went home and other stragglers took their places. But Borden, Johnson and Walker, all young and full of adventure, determined to stay it out. They went over to the Bernard, which flows almost midway between the Brazos and Colorado and tramped through the deep woods with their heavy draperies of dull gray moss, and noting the splendid alluvial soil determined that here in these woods was the place that they would choose for their habitation.

James Cummings and Sylvanus Castleman had selected their sections on the Colorado. James H. Bell fancied a site on the Brazos.

Some of the Colonists had brought horses with them and some of them were fortunate enough to have captured a horse from the wild herds that abounded, but it required great skill to do this and most of them tramped hither and yon on foot while herds of splendid horses scampered away across the prairie at their approach.

A second summer was well advanced before the first news was received from Austin. A messenger came up the Colorado and across the Brazos to tell that Austin would be at the house of Sylvanus Castleman on the Colorado the first Sunday in August and had asked that all the Colonists in that vicinity assemble there and hear his message. Thomas H. Borden was among those who foregathered.

Austin and the old Baron de Bastrop had been commissioned by the Mexican authorities to act as commissioners to organize and instruct the Colonists and issue them titles for their land. The old Baron who had lived at San Antonio for a great many years and had been in the Spanish service, was now in the Mexican

The Old Three Hundred

service, a second alcalde for the municipality of Bexar. He was a man seven feet in height and then nearly eighty years old. In his younger days he had been an officer in the celebrated giant regiment of Frederick the Great. In his later days he had been a refugee from Holland to Louisiana and then a refugee from Louisiana to Texas when Louisiana was acquired by the French at the close of the last century.

When the Colonists were assembled at Sylvanus Castleman's they were told that instead of one section of land to a single man and two sections to a family, that each family could have a league and a labor; that a single man could have half a league; that if a Colonist should marry a Mexican woman he would have an additional allowance. Here was bounty to a high degree. They had asked for sections and had been given leagues and labors and any Colonist who would marry a Mexican woman should have a fourth of a league added as a dowry. It was necessary for each Colonist to select his site and the land would have to be surveyed and the field notes of these surveys carefully checked and returned, after which the title would issue. This new arrangement substituting leagues for sections upset their plans and made it necessary for them to have more elbow-room.

Since Austin was authorized to make three hundred grants he required three hundred separate surveys, and surveyors were immediately appointed to go out with the settlers and make the essential locations. Thomas H. Borden was one of those appointed by Austin to make these first surveys. He and Johnson and Walker at once organized themselves into a surveying party not only for the purpose of locating their own land but locating land for others. Horatio Chrisman, Ira Ingram and others with surveying talent were at once employed in this enterprise and surveying parties scattered all along the lower Colorado and Brazos and as far east as the Trinity and San Jacinto Bay.

The lands desired were, of course, those on the water courses. Each league was given a minimum front of one fourth of its depth on the waterway and was to run back about five miles for distance. No league could be located within ten miles of the Gulf coast, so beginning back at this distance nearly three hundred league surveys and as many labors were located during the ensuing year along the banks of these rivers, each Colonist selecting his site as his fancy dictated.

Selection of sites for leagues and labors was quite different from a location for mere sections and many of those who had wondered about and made tentative locations during the long year of waiting while Austin was in Mexico had to revise their plans. A section was only a square mile while a league was more than seven square miles. Settlers living on contiguous sections

The Old Three Hundred

would be near each other, while if living on a vast domain of seven square miles they would be remote. There was great hurrying and trading and changing during the entire year to expand the sections into leagues and each man found himself fighting for elbow-room, although they were squirming in an area as vast as New England.

Since all of these surveyors spoke English and most of them English only, they made their original surveys and field notes in the English language and wrote them upon odd scraps of paper, after which they were carefully translated into Spanish.

After Austin and Bastrop had given the Colonists full instructions and they had been set to work surveying their lands, they sought out a site for a town which was to be the official headquarters of the Colony and found it at a place on a high west bank of the Brazos about one hundred miles from its mouth and called it San Felipe de Austin. Here the Empresario built a cabin and opened his office and it remained the Capitol of the Colonies until its destruction during the Revolution in 1836.

Thomas H. Borden, who was one of the official surveyors for the first and for subsequent Colonial grants, spent much of his time at San Felipe and had a residence there after his marriage in 1829.

In July, 1824, a year after Bastrop's first

visit he was back on the Colorado and the Brazos and delivered titles, grants all written on imperishable parchment and written in very formal Spanish language to each Colonist. Johnson, Borden and Walker, who had combined their claims, got a league on the lower Bernard.

The Mortons, who had stopped and planted and harvested on the north rim of the river across from the fort and big bend, were conceded first choice; William Morton, who had a family with him and daughters, chose a two league grant which was graciously made him and which was located on the north margin of the river just across from where the prosperous little city of Richmond now stands.

Thomas H. Borden, who was now an official surveyor, had wanted to locate his grant on the river next to the big bend, but Randal Jones, who had been in the country long before Austin came, claimed the next preference and it was conceded him.

James Knight and Walter C. White and others who had preceded Thomas H. Borden, indicated preferences which took up the entire outer rim of the bend and there was not sufficient land in the bend to permit the location of a league.

Tom Borden made the official survey of Morton's land and other contiguous surveys, and all the while cherished the notion that some

The Old Three Hundred

day he would buy land and have his home there.

These folks, including Thomas H. Borden, had all learned in the year's residence that the land inside the bend, though less fertile than that across, was not subject to overflow and when the great river left its banks and spread over the vast alluvial lands on the north and east, the high antediluvian sand-bar was still dry. This led these leaguers who had made locations across the river to apply for their appurtenant labors inside the bend. So for the time being Tom gave up his dream of a league and labor here at the great bend and William Morton, William Little, Randal Jones, James Knight and Walter C. White and William Andrews, all of whom had located their leagues across the river, located their labors inside the bend, each living on his 177 acres. This made the first compact settlement in Colonial Texas. They got their labors at the same time they got title to their leagues in July, 1824, and Knight and White at once established a trading station. This was now and afterwards called the Fort Settlement and assumed an air of social and commercial importance.

Big Jesse Thompson, whom Tom and Gail Borden had met in New Orleans on their first advent there, had come as one of the Old Three Hundred and had located his league down in Brazoria. He visited the bend during the idle summer of 1822 and saw its possibilities, and in 1827 he purchased an option on the Knight and White labor No. 6 and bought land across the river and began preparations to establish his residence here and open a plantation. In due time he built a commodious house across the river and one of his sons had a home in the bend on the Knight and White labor. He began negotiations to buy out the holdings of the other residents of the bend and had visions not unlike those of Thomas H. Borden to own the bend and live on it near his ample plantation across the river. But Jesse Thompson was a shrewd trader and took his time in his dealings with his neighbors. He wanted a bargain. He established a ferry across the river and there was a kind of highway running east and west which crossed here.

When Tom Borden, who never gave up his ambition to own land in the bend, renewed his efforts in that direction a few years later it brought a serious conflict with Jesse Thompson.

Two hundred ninety-seven titles were surveyed and issued by Austin and the old Baron in July, 1824, and the Colonists now on their leagues and labors went to work with might and main. To hew their houses out of the woods and dig their living out of the soil and defend themselves against the lurking Karankawa Indians and overcome the innumerable hardships of a frontier life, presented many dif-

The Old Three Hundred

ficulties, but these difficulties never daunted them. They considered themselves prosperous and were happy, and Tom Borden now began to write back to Gail in Mississippi and his family in Indiana praising the opportunities of Texas. He did not, however, advise that Gail give up his life in Mississippi and join him in Texas just yet for he feared that the hardships that he was enduring would be too much for his more delicate brother. But the reports which came from Texas during these years from Colonists who had located here caused hundreds of others to come hither. Austin secured permission to found four more Colonies and other Empresarios came, so that during the years from 1824 to 1832 there were numerous settlements all the way from the Guadalupe to the Sabine and a population of nearly twenty thousand people had come into Texas from the Southern States.

The attitude of the Colonists toward Mexico during these years is well told in a letter which Ira Ingram, who had settled on Matagorda Bay, wrote his Uncle Roswell in Michigan in 1830. "We have nothing to fear and daily enjoy more to create deep gratitude toward the government of our adopted country than any other people on earth. We have received donations of the richest land on earth in one of the loveliest climates in the world. We elect all our officers, civil and military, are exempt from all taxes, are situated well to carry on commerce with the world, have liveoak enough to rebuild all the ships of the world." To this he might have added that the Mexican government had paid the Colonists the high compliment of offering their daughters as wives and a landed dowry with each bride.

All those who came were not as happy over the situation as Ira Ingram and Thomas H. Borden. Some said that Texas was a land of eternal hardships. Those who viewed it with the optimism of Ira Ingram saw much more in it than those who succumbed to its hardships and went back to the States with a story of failure.

The varied reports from Texas during these years indicated that it was a land of plenty or a land of poverty. It abounded in wealth of almost every character but wealth that had to be reduced to possession. It was a land where thousands of beautiful horses galloped over the terrain which was decorated with everlasting flowers, but the weary settler walked on his long journeys trudging to and fro unable to get a mount. In a land which could produce endless fields of cotton he dressed himself in the skins of such animals as he could kill. In a land which could produce endless fields of corn he was compelled to live on meat and often then on horse-meat.

It was a land of eternal sunshine and one

of awful winter. Frequently after the long summers the winters would be so mild that roses would bloom from year to year and no frost would fall as far south as the coast. Then came a terrible winter in which Galveston Bay was frozen over and a bear crossed on the ice. Thomas H. Borden long told a story illustrating these contrasts in the case of a pioneer who was driving his ox-team across the prairie in the late autumn. The sunshine beat down on the plain and the heat was so intense that one of the oxen was overcome and died from it. The thrifty settler thought to save the hide of the beast and set to work skinning it. While he was so employed a norther suddenly blew up and the other ox was frozen to death. It was a land of drought and the land of rainfall; in one season there would be sixty inches of rainfall and the rivers would overflow. Thomas H. Borden once wrote Moses Lapham of Columbia that he had been waterbound four days by a rain which had not ceased morning, noon or night. Then again the droughts would be so severe that the corn crops would be destroyed; that there would be no grain for man or beast, the prairies would be so dry that fires would sweep over them.

It was a land of peace—it was a land of war. One could wander throughout the entire confines of the Colonies from the San Jacinto to the Lavaca without meeting a hostile demonstration; all nature seemed at peace. The Colonist rarely ever had a lock on his door. Then without warning the Karankawas would come out of the swamps along the coast and spread death and desolation to the isolated Colonists.

It was an English land—it was a Spanish land. For three hundred years Spain had been the overlord of this country, though during that time it had never reduced any part of it to possession except the small confines about San Antonio and the San Antonio River and at the small settlement at Nacogdoches in east Texas. Despite this the laws of the Colonies were Spanish laws that had been imported into Mexico from Spain by the conquerors three hundred years ago. Not only were all the laws of Coahuila and Texas written in Spanish but every transaction had to be done in Spanish. The land titles issued to the Colonists bore Spanish terms which they could not understand. Yet all the Colonists spoke English, wrote English, thought English and gradually introduced into the country the manners and customs, as well as the laws of their English ancestors.

It was a Catholic land—it was a Protestant land. The grant to Moses Austin that was subsequently confirmed to his son permitted him to bring three hundred families from Louisiana—they were to be Catholics and

The Old Three Hundred

no other religion was to be permitted. Outwardly they were Catholics. Austin publicly professed that religion, though he privately wrote criticisms of it in his diary. Sam Houston, who came to Texas a few years later, was baptized in the Catholic church. But in spite of this ninety-nine per cent of the people were Protestants and pioneer preachers from the States soon began to permeate the country and spread the "true gospel." But as Ira Ingram wrote his Uncle Roswell, the religious requirements of Austin's grant did not materially interfere with the Colonists' religion.

Matrimony was a problem for the young men—women were at a premium. While the Mexican nation encouraged marriages with native women, there were no native women in Colonial Texas and it was a long way to Mexico where they could be found. At San Antonio, which was a Mexican City of some few thousand souls there were plenty of them and hundreds of Americans who went there in those years succumbed to the charms of Mexican feminine beauty. But as far as we know, Tom Borden never went there. Nor did he go back to the States. His idea was well expressed in a letter he wrote Moses Lapham a few years later, that a Texan should marry a woman "who was broke to the climate." In 1829, after he had been seven years in the country and when many people were coming from everywhere a family named Woodward came from Connecticut and there was a daughter, Demis Woodward, and in that year she became the wife of Thomas H. Borden.

Marriage in those days in Texas must be solemnized by a priest but there was no resident priest in the lower settlements and it was permitted as perfectly proper that the contracting parties could solemnize their vows with a simple contract and later when the priest came along on his periodical journey for marriages and baptisms he could perform a belated ceremony and perhaps at the same time there could be a christening.

Father Muldoon usually made the rounds twice each year for these events and such other spiritual administration as seemed necessary.

It may be that Demis Woodward was beautiful and that Tom Borden's courtship was ardent and romantic. All we know of her is a dim tradition. Her two little boys were only three and five when she died in October, 1836. Moses Lapham, who was much in the Borden home during these years, wrote his father in Ohio that she was a woman of great charm and with many womanly virtues.

Chapter V

THE BORDENS GO TO TEXAS

Gail Borden, Jr. found life easy and led a happy existence during his six years in Amite County, Mississippi. He fell easily into the changed ways of these Southern folks who were kindly to him. He was a charming personality and during his long life no man ever spoke ill of him. His integrity was never questioned, yet he was not easy going for he had a mind that was ever active. During the first two years he spent much of the time out of doors and the genial Southern winters were much more kindly to him than the more extreme frost of the Indiana woods had been. Between surveying in the summer season and teaching in the winter season and reading the year around the ample books that he found in the Green Valley library, he spent six very profitable years and largely supplied the deficiency that existed because of his meager schooling.

Along with his surveying, teaching and reading, however, he employed himself in another useful enterprise. He fell in love, courted and married.

About fifty years after Roger Williams, the great Baptist preacher, was exiled from the Massachusetts colony and walked his way through the winter to Rhode Island where he founded the Colony that afterwards became the State, and spread the gospel according to the Baptist ritual, a family of Mercers from the Virginia colonies found their way into North Carolina. Here early in the Eighteenth Century Silas Mercer was born and one of his sons Jesse, born shortly after the middle of the century, became the great Southern Baptist preacher and evangelist of his day. The Reverend Jesse Mercer found his way in boyhood to Georgia where from his earliest manhood he preached Christ and Him crucified and taught the efficacy of

The Bordens Go to Texas

baptism as an essential to salvation. He was the outstanding Baptist minister of his day in Georgia, if not the entire South, and spent much of his life in missionary work and was the founder of Mercer University now at Macon, Georgia.

Another of old Silas' sons and a brother of Jesse was the Reverend Thomas Mercer, who though equally fervent in spreading the cause of the Lord, was not as famous as his distinguished Georgia brother. The Reverend Thomas had a son by the name of Eli, who, in his very young manhood, removed to Amite County, Mississippi, and when only twenty-two married Nancy Tomson, a girl of fifteen, and they lived in the little town of Liberty in Amite County when Gail Borden made his appearance there. Their oldest daughter, Penelope, was only ten when Gail Borden began to teach school at Liberty and for a time she was one of his pupils. During the six years of his residence she grew from a school girl to a very beautiful young woman and in December, 1828, she and Gail Borden, Jr. were married.

Whatever prejudice, if any, Gail may have had against the institution of slavery when he lived up in the Indiana woods seems to have been dissipated by his residence in Mississippi, for the records at Liberty show that in January, 1828, before his marriage to Penelope the following December he purchased a slave girl by the name of Ellen at public auction. Evidently he was contemplating the necessity of a housemaid when he made the purchase. The union in faraway southwest Mississippi of these two descendants of outstanding Baptist families seemed an orthodox thing.

The good reports coming from Texas during these years, chiefly those sent by Thomas H. Borden, aroused the Mercers and the Bordens of Liberty, Mississippi, as well as the Bordens back in Indiana, to migrate to Texas. Gail Borden, Sr., the father, with his wife and daughter and two sons, left Indiana early in 1829. At Memphis where they stopped en route, the mother and infant daughter died and the remnant of the broken family journeyed on down to New Orleans.

In the autumn of 1829 Eli Mercer, with his wife and five children and their slaves, ten people in all, left for Texas, traveling by boat to Natchitoches, Louisiana, and overland by wagon where they reached the Colorado in what is now Wharton County at a place then called Egypt, on the 29th of November in that year.

Gail Borden and his wife, Penelope, went to New Orleans where they met his father and minor brother John P. and Paschal Pavalo, the third brother, and all of them together took the boat for Galveston, reaching there in December, 1829.

The Bordens Go to Texas

The day after the boat reached Galveston a daughter was born to Gail and Penelope and they named her Mary.

After a very short stay in Galveston they went to the mouth of the Colorado where they were joined by Thomas H. Borden and journeyed to Egypt where they joined the Mercers. Here at Egypt on the Colorado, Gail Borden, Jr. and his family lived for the next three years.

Coming as Colonists they were all entitled to land grants and the ample and liberal provisions that had obtained when Austin's first Colonists came were still effective in 1829. Thomas H. Borden, who had now become one of the established surveyors in the Colony, could easily tell them how to get their land and they proceeded promptly to do so. Thomas, who had gotten one-third of a league as a single man in 1824, hurried to relate his marital status to the government and got another half league. There was a league for the father, Gail Borden, Sr., a league for Gail, Jr. and his wife Penelope, a half league for the blacksmith brother, Paschal Pavalo, and one for Eli Mercer—about 20,000 acres all for the asking.

Tom Borden still had his eye on the big bend country and Gail's league was located on the nearest available land about ten miles above it.

Gail, Jr. spent most of the years, 1830-32 at Egypt on the Colorado where he tried farming but was soon on Austin's staff of surveyors and his careful clerical work was sought by Austin whom he aided in keeping his voluminous land records. Like Thomas H., he acquired a residence at San Felipe and was soon deep in the social, political and economic life of the Colonies. He bought a town lot in San Felipe for which he paid $30.00 and was Sergeant of Militia. He and Thomas H. were away much of the time, surveying for Austin all the way from Bastrop to the Bay.

In 1831 a most likely young man named Moses Lapham left college in Oxford, Ohio, and his father's family at Mechanicsburg and found his way to San Felipe where his genteel bearing won him the friendship of the Bordens and he became a member of their clan, was soon inducted into their far-flung surveying work and was much of the time an inmate of Thomas H. Borden's household. His first letter home avowed that "It appears to be a very clever family and I have been treated with much kindness so far." Although Moses was pleased with the Bordens he could not say much for society generally at San Felipe. He wrote, "It is such as to preclude any satisfaction. I stay about a mile from town. Spend my time when not at work reading, while the townspeople are gambling, swearing and fighting as their chief amusements."

Paschal Pavalo opened a blacksmith shop,

The Bordens Go to Texas

and the whole family was now deeply engaged in varied avocations.

One evening late in the autumn the local peace officer came to Paschal's shop with a prisoner and asked the blacksmith to fabricate handcuffs and chains for the miscreant who was to be held until he could be sent down to Saltillo, the Capital of Coahuila and Texas, for trial for murder. Borden recognized the man as one Parker, who had been drifting about the Colonies for a year or more, and who had a past which was only told in whispers. His name was not Parker at all. He was the son of one of the great Governors of Kentucky and twenty years before, while his good old father was Governor, he had committed a heinous murder for which he was under sentence to be hanged. All other avenues closed, the anguished father wrote a pardon for the son and with the same pen, his own resignation as Governor. While in jail the culprit had tried to cut his throat and had made a bad job of it so that he ever after wore a metal tube as an aid to his windpipe. At San Felipe he had fallen in with a former Kentucky acquaintance who had a wallet full of money and was in Texas to buy horses. Parker had lured the horse buyer into the woods and murdered him against the peace and dignity of the commonwealth of Coahuila and Texas. There was no jail in San Felipe so he was well ironed and turned over to Uncle Jimmie Whitesides, the tavern keeper, to be held awaiting his extradition. A week later cholera broke out in San Felipe and Uncle Jimmie reported his prisoner dead and buried, and the incident was forgotten. A year later Big Jesse Thompson met Parker in Mobile and when he reported the matter back home they dug up Uncle Jimmie's "corpse" and found a block of wood. No one cared much and the incident was again closed. Fifty years later it was reported that this miscreant had made his way to the Islands of the Pacific and become a respectable citizen and left a highly respectable family. In 1928 I visited these Islands and corroborated this statement where I found sons and grandsons of Parker still living—nearly forty people—who were his descendants by a native woman he had married in 1850—splendid folks bearing the proud name of the old Governor which Parker had disclosed to them on his death-bed.

The Bordens went into the woods at San Felipe and cut logs with which to build their homes, and Moses Lapham, who helped them, wrote of the event and told that he had cut his foot in the enterprise.

Life in Texas in these days was primitive and it took all Gail Borden's time to make a living for his fast increasing family and he was never idle and even now he pondered inventions in a vague way. Noah Smithwick, who had a blacksmith shop near the Borden's, left a statement

The Bordens Go to Texas

that Gail Borden's inventive genius was working during these years, but he added that it was not a mechanical success.

The Bordens were clannish, the family tie was very strong with them and they had great plans for various ventures to be launched in Texas. Thomas Henry, who because of his long residence here and his wide acquaintance with men and affairs, took the lead in the family councils. He had never given up the idea of a plantation and a gin, a town, even a city at Fort Bend, or the Fort Settlement as it was called. So late in the '20s he began to buy up the several labors, the small tracts that had been located in the bend by the two Littles, William Morton and Randal Jones. He would build a city here and call it Louisville and he wrote this to Moses Lapham, who had gone back to Ohio. "My next letter to you will be from Louisville. Address me there. I am living there now and have built a gin and last year raised and ginned thirty bales of cotton and four hundred bushels of sweet potatoes." The antediluvian sand-bar was fertile ground for sweet potatoes.

His home was now in the Fort Settlement, although much of his time was spent at San Felipe and on far frontiers where he was locating land in Austin's fourth and fifth Colonies.

But Big Jesse Thompson had preceded him to the Bend and had bought labor No. 6 from Knight and White and had been dickering with other settlers for their labors. He did not like the intrusion and made very free talk about Thomas Henry and sent him a warning that the Bend, though ten miles in circumference, was too small for both of them. Besides Big Jesse had two grown sons who were formidable fellows and who shared their father's views about the Borden intrusion. There was ugly talk and there were threats. Finally some of the Fort Settlement neighbors offered their good offices to bring about a reconciliation, and a formal truce was made. It was written and signed and read:

"We agree that our dispute is about to be left to gentlemen, we will cease hostile movements towards each other, as also the members of our respective family. Signed in the presence of R. Jones. (Signed) J. Thompson. Thos. H. Borden."

This seemed a happy ending of the community feud and peace was promised

What really happened is hard to reconstruct after the lapse of more than one hundred years. There was no newspaper published in Texas at that time and the court records are silent. A granddaughter of Jesse Thompson, who in 1936 still owned the Knight and White labor No. 6, says that Tom Borden assassinated her grandfather.

Thomas H. Borden on March 8, 1835, wrote his friend Moses Lapham, who was then in Ohio the following circumstantial account:

The Bordens Go to Texas

"Thompson delayed calling the board . . . I had business at one of the nabours and went by Thompsons and on my way back one of his boys shot at me with a rifle. Thompson, the old man, was below (down the river) and when he came home in a day or two he made no apology to me. I started to go to San Felipe with a two horse wagon. James Cochran was with me, who Thompson had also threatened. I had proceeded two miles when we were surprised by Thompson and one Dr. Erwin coming up to me with a large pistol in his hand and says, 'I have got you, damn you.' I was on the ground where I had gotten to mind a trace. I had a small pistol in my side-pocket—the rest of my arms were in the wagon. I drew and fired at Thompson and at the same time he fired at me but we both missed. My horses ran off to the timber three hundred yards away and I went after them and got my big pistols and a double-barrel shotgun and got on my best horse and went back to see what had become of James Cochran. When I first saw them they were in a scuffle or fight and I fired, but Cochran grabbed the muzzle and then I shot the old rascal . . . He lived three hours and I went to town and gave up and am now under $2500.00 bond."

This is all the evidence available of the grim tragedy in the Big Bend on a March day one hundred years ago.

Big Jesse's sons, Hiram and Jesse, continued

to live there for many years and to operate the ferry, and Thos. H. Borden continued to live there for a decade. He still cherished the idea of a city of Louisville and for a year gave his letters a date line under that name

John P., the youngest Borden, was twenty-three and it was deemed wise to have him taught Spanish, so he was sent to San Antonio and boarded with a Mexican family at an expense of $22.00 per month and studied the soft poetic language. They ran some risk in exposing this fine handsome six foot youngster to the charms of Mexican beauties in Bexar. James Bowie, Deaf Smith, Phil Dimmitt, Horatio Alsberry and a host of others who had been so exposed in recent years had taken Mexican wives. But the handsome Borden youngster was soon at war and a year later Moses Lapham wrote home: "I was at John P. Borden's wedding a short time since. There were many fine looking young ladies there who danced well and sang well, but the Southern customs prevented anything like approaching near enough to hear them converse." One must suspect that young Lapham was a timid youth.

But he adds, "I must give the people of the Colorado credit for their unexampled good behavior. There was not a single person in the whole assembly who appeared the least intoxicated."

Among the other enterprises on hand with

The Bordens Go to Texas

the Bordens, in addition to their plantations and gin and surveying and blacksmith shop, and John's venture into Spanish, was a try at journalism. Gail, Jr. and Thomas H. started a newspaper. There had been a weekly paper at San Felipe for nearly four years, but it had ceased to function and the press had been removed to Brazoria. Thomas H. went to New Orleans and bought a Smith medium hand press and the two Bordens with Joseph H. (Don Jose) Baker, under the firm name of Baker & Borden, perfected all arrangements to begin the publication of the Texas Telegraph and Register in October, 1835, which became the press of the Revolution, the official organ of the three governments which followed each other in quick succession, and for nearly forty years continued the leading paper in Texas.

They were versatile men, these Bordens, and Gail Borden's mind never rested. He had one of those rare intellects that was forever working, exploring, trying new fields, and journalism seemed a fitting outlet for such a mentality.

Chapter VI

GAIL BORDEN HELPS WRITE THE FIRST TEXAS CONSTITUTION

While Mexico did not impose an ad valorem tax on the lands it had given the Colonists, some twenty million acres, it did make a gesture toward imposing a tariff, and a rude Customs House had been built on the end of Galveston Island, though there was yet no town there, and another up at the east end of Galveston Bay

Gail Borden and the First Texas Constitution

at the mouth of the Trinity at a place called Anahuac, and another at the mouth of the Brazos. But the Colonists had been spoiled and the merchants who brought in goods did not want to pay these import taxes. A garrison of soldiers had been stationed at the mouth of the Brazos under Colonel Domingo de Ugartechea, an educated Mexican gentleman, and another at Anahuac under Colonel John Davis Bradburn, a renegade American from Tennessee and another under Colonel Piedras at Nacogdoches, a jolly poker playing cadet. The Mexican soldiers sent to these remote garrisons were recruited from the jails and by and large were undesirable fellows. When these collectors of customs came to impose duties, they did not have dependable schedules and generally took whatever they could get.

The Texans were not allowed to raise tobacco, the monopoly on this franchise being enjoyed by one of the southern Mexican States, and a thriving contraband trade soon sprung up in this "filthy weed" and cargoes from the southern States would land at the easy Texas ports and go overland across the Rio Grande.

There was a minority of hot headed fellows in Texas who, from the day they came, were against Mexican authority and for the independence of Texas. It was easy to make trouble between them and these garrisons. But it is worthy of note that the trouble did not begin with Colonel Ugartechea or Colonel Piedras, but with the swashbuckling Tennessee refugee from justice, Colonel Bradburn at Anahuac. In 1832 the Texans drove out Bradburn and with the momentum thus aroused extended the expulsion act to the other garrisons.

Mexico at this hour was in the midst of one of its revolutions fomented by General Santa Anna, a candidate for President, and the "rebellion" in Texas was overlooked for the time being and the "rebels" made haste to declare their allegiance to this champion of liberty and constitutional rights. The conservative element in Texas headed by Austin and embracing all the Bordens deplored this strife and made haste to give assurances of loyalty to Mexico. To prove this they called a convention in 1832 and restated their undying fealty to the good mother country; but they had some grievances which they desired to discuss.

At this San Felipe Convention, which was the first held by the Colonists, they pointed out that Texas was now fit for statehood and that they desired to be separated from the Mexican State of Coahuila to which they had been attached as a kind of outlying territory. In genteel respectful terms they petitioned the supreme powers down in Mexico to consider these things and give them a local state government more suitable to their needs.

When news of this gathering reached Mexi-

Gail Borden and the First Texas Constitution

can officialdom it was received with grave suspicion and taken as an act of secession. The Spanish mind could not grasp a situation in which men would meet to peacefully discuss such problems. All such gatherings with them were per se seditious. They could no more visualize a lawful gathering of this kind than they could a peaceful fight or a legal mob. All south of the Rio Grande the supreme powers "knitted their brows like the gathering storm, nursing their wrath to keep it warm."

The Jefe Politico at San Antonio writing his superiors down in Mexico advised that these rebellious spirits be driven from the country.

But the Colonists on the Colorado and the Brazos were oblivious of the bad impression made by their 1832 Convention and held another one there in 1833 in which they went a step further. They not only petitioned for separate statehood but actually drew up a constitution for the separate state to be, and sent it down to Mexico along with their petition.

Eli Mercer was a delegate to the first Convention in 1832, and Gail Borden was present as a spectator and was a delegate to the second in 1833 and helped write the first of the seven constitutions of Texas.

There were some interesting men in this Convention whom Borden met for the first time. Among the delegates was a tall, powerful looking, dissipated looking man who registered from

Nacogdoches, but who was in fact a resident of the Cherokee Indian reservation in western Arkansas from where he had come via Nacogdoches to attend this gathering. His name was Sam Houston and he had lately been Governor of Tennessee, and it was whispered that he was present at the instance of the President of the United States. The year before he had visited Texas under a passport from the Secretary of War of the United States and had written President Jackson a long personal letter suggesting it would be easy for the United States to acquire Texas and advising that a convention of all Texas was to be held next year (1833) which he would attend.

After this first trip he had gone back to his wigwam and firewater and waited for the time to attend the 1833 gathering. After it he again went back to his savage habitation, but he came again and to stay in 1834. He was deeply laying plans for a "comeback" which he executed with consummate skill.

There was a delegate from up the river named Nestor Clay, a nephew of the great Henry Clay, who looked still more dissipated than delegate Houston, and who until he got helplessly drunk on the second day charmed the Convention with his brilliant presence.

The presiding officer of the 1833 Convention was the young and gifted William H. Wharton, who was Gail Borden's age and who

Gail Borden and the First Texas Constitution

was the open enemy of the great Austin whose conservatism he despised and whose prestige he envied.

When the Convention had finished its labors the English draft of the petition and the proposed constitution for the proposed state were translated into Spanish and Austin was delegated to take them to Mexico for presentation, and as he had done twelve years before he took the long, long trail.

He had much to do before he could get away for what he thought was a three months absence, and Gail Borden who had worked for him and with him helped day and night until he left on horseback in April. His last injunction to Borden as he rode away was, "For God's sake do not let my people do anything foolish or rash while I am away."

Gail watched him disappear down the Columbia highway little dreaming it would be two and one-half years before his return.

During all this long time Gail Borden was in charge of Austin's office at San Felipe answering all correspondence, making surveys giving field notes, issuing titles to lands. When requests for surveys and land locations would come in he would either go in person and make them or send his brother Tom.

A letter from a man in Brazoria asks, "When can Tom survey the lands on the Navidad?"

An engineer and mapmaker at New Orleans

wrote him to ask that he furnish him a dependable map of Texas. "I want a better and more dependable one than any now extant in the United States," he wrote. All the while Borden was at work on the map of Texas he was getting out for Austin, which was not completed until after Austin's death a year later.

The Bordens, in fact all Texans, were strong believers in constitutional government. They felt that the time had come in human affairs when Democracy bound by constitutional covenants could carry on. When the Texans first came in 1822-1824, Mexico was in the thraldom of change. Santa Anna, a young Vera Cruz Lieutenant, declaring for a Democracy, had started the revolt which sounded the death knell of Iturbide's empire. When it fell, patriotic men like Victoria had drafted and adopted the Mexican constitution of 1824. Stephen F. Austin, who was in the confidence of these men had furnished a suggestive draft which was used in its preparation.

Santa Anna had no part in all this but was scheming to seize the vacant throne of Iturbide.

In the ten years which followed there were almost constant civil wars between the factions down in Mexico usually fomented by Santa Anna, the arch schemer who posed always as a champion of popular institutions.

These wars did not reach Texas which was far away and depended little on Mexican rela-

Gail Borden and the First Texas Constitution

tionships. The people here wanted to be let alone and were opening their plantations establishing markets and fighting the Indians. All they wanted in 1833 was a state government which was nearer home and a code of statutes suitable to their needs and a tribunal where they could try their criminals without sending them all the way to Saltillo.

Santa Anna had realized a ten year ambition in 1832 when by military force he had driven out President Bustamante, who had driven out Guerrero, who had driven out Pedraza, the last lawful President. Declaring for a Democracy and a constitution when he overthrew the Empire in 1823, he had repeated the ruse when he attacked Bustamante in 1832 whom he charged was "addicted to centralizm." And now he was the President of Mexico and had subscribed to the oath to support the constitution. In far away Texas he was hailed as a deliverer—a tribune of the people.

Elected upon promises of reform which would have impinged upon the aristocracy and the clergy and which he had no notion of performing, El Presidente had retired to his plantation leaving Gomez Farias, his Vice-President, in charge while he plotted the coup by which he would overthrow the constitution he had sworn to observe, dismantle the state governments, assume dictorial powers and rule Mexico according to his own notions.

Gail Borden, Pioneer

It was into this foul atmosphere reeking with reactionary germs that the saintly, sincere Austin came in 1833, bearing the first constitution of Texas. He was about as welcome as a skunk at a lawn party. They kept him hanging around for six months and after he had in despair departed for home and ridden as far as Saltillo he was arrested, returned to Mexico and incarcerated in a deep, dark dungeon left over from the Inquisition.

In the meantime some of Austin's people at home had done some of the foolish things which he had feared in his parting admonition to Gail Borden.

But it was not the Bordens or the Whartons, the bona fide homeseekers and planters, as we shall see.

Saltillo in Coahuila was the Capital of Coahuila and Texas, but the State was now torn into factions one of which sought to remove the Capital to Monclova, and Governor Augustine Viesca, a man of easy virtue, was holding forth there in 1834 and 1835 and mock sessions of the Legislature now and then met there. Certain enterprising persons from the United States, aided by leading citizens of Texas, foregathered there at these sessions and prevailed on Governor Viesca and his Legislators to make them vast land grants in Texas for more than one thousand leagues of land on one pretext or another. Among these grants was one to three

Gail Borden and the First Texas Constitution

Texans—Francis White Johnson, Dr. Peebles and Samuel M. Williams, who covenanted with the Governor that for four hundred leagues of land they would repair to Texas and raise a regiment of a thousand men and put them at his disposal for the protection of the frontier and such other purposes as he might need the aid of an army. They were left free to bargain with each soldier enlisted the amount of land he should receive for his services.

On a day in July, 1835 these three worthy gentlemen, Empresarios as they were called, were back in San Felipe bringing with them all in Spanish and bearing seals and official signatures the contract with the Governor and bringing also blank certificates to issue to these soldiers to be enlisted.

On the night of July 5th they issued twenty-seven of these certificates for ten leagues each to twenty-seven persons, each certificate reciting that the person to whom issued had enlisted as a soldier under the terms of the contract. A week later they issued thirteen more, so that for four hundred leagues they had enlisted forty soldiers.

One of these certificates was issued to Gail Borden and one each to his brothers Paschal and John P., and within a few weeks surveys were made and all the forty ten-league grants located in deep East Texas, and the second Alcalde of Nacogdoches, Radford Berry, made out grants to the holders of the certificates.

Gail Borden, Pioneer

Just why these guilty Empresarios who had gotten four hundred leagues of land (178,000 acres) to equip a thousand men in arms should have fled from Monclova to San Felipe and hurriedly passed it in ten league blocks to forty men, was never known. John P. Borden, who was Commissioner of the General Land Office of the Republic in 1840, told an investigating committee of the Fifth Congress that he never knew of the grant to him until long after it was made; that he was never consulted about it. Neither Gail, Jr. nor Paschal ever claimed the ten leagues conveyed to them, and it may be assumed they knew no more about it than John P.

Texans had never paid any ad valorem taxes, and by virtue of this exemption they had declined to observe the revenue laws. The lonely little Mexican Custom House on the end of Galveston Island had cobwebs on the door.

The Mexican garrisons had been driven out in 1832 and now in 1834 more were being sent to enforce these dead-letter excise regulations. One of them was at Anahuac. Burning with patriotic fervor, Colonel William B. Travis, who eight months later died at the Alamo, raised a company of volunteers and went down to Anahuac, captured the Mexican garrison and took them one and all up to Harrisburg where they were entertained at a Fourth of July picnic and allowed to go back to Mexico.

Gail Borden and the First Texas Constitution

The authorities down in Mexico easily seized on these overt acts as an excuse for an aggression against the people of Texas.

All during the summer of 1834 Texas patriots with bogus land certificates in their pockets, knowing that they were done for if Santa Anna's soldiers reached Texas, were riding up and down the land preaching war. Austin was yet in prison and there was no leader to take his place. Ninety per cent of the people of Texas, those who owned their homes and had no part in the land frauds or in flouting the revenue laws, were for peace, and at first took little part in the call to arms. They did not know what was going on down in Mexico, did not know of the deep laid plans of Santa Anna.

Released from prison Austin returned home in September and all Texas waited to hear his advice. Gail Borden at San Felipe, hearing of his return, said, "If Colonel Austin is for war we are for war, if he is for peace, we are for peace." He knew they would depend on Austin's judgment and that he knew better than anyone what was going on down in Mexico.

Gail, and his brother John P., rode down from San Felipe to see Austin, who was resting a few days at the home of his sister at Peach Point below Brazoria and sat on the veranda in the soft September sea breeze and talked long hours with him. He had no patience with the land grabbing patriots nor with those who were flouting Mexican revenue laws nor did the Bordens, but Austin told them much more was at stake, that it was a question of despotism versus constitutional government. The Austins and the Bordens and other large land owners who had their ample holdings as bounties from a generous government could easily make their peace with official Mexico and give up the persons who had been guilty of the land frauds and who had defied the revenue laws, but they must realize now that the price of this security was submission to a despot. These great-grandsons of Roger Williams did not have to be argued with on this issue. One might as well have asked them to give up the Baptist church or baptism by emersion or surrender the Roger Williams Bible as to barter away the constitution. They were for war, or whatever the cost to protect the great principle, and to war they went.

CHAPTER VII

THE BORDENS GO TO WAR

When Austin returned to Texas in September he found the State sharply divided between what was called the War Party and the Peace Party. A large element of the so-called War Party were those who had numerous land certificates that would be outlawed by Santa Anna's government. And there were those who had been active in violating the revenue laws and for whom the military authorities in Mexico held warrants for arrest. There was on the other hand a Peace Party, as always, that wanted peace at any price.

The Bordens and possibly the majority of the people of Texas, wanted to hear what Austin had to say and were willing to go to war if necessary to protect the fundamental principles of constitutional government. Austin at this hour held the destiny of Texas in his hand.

On the evening of September 8, 1835, he was tendered a dinner at Brazoria and delivered what might be called a keynote speech in which he cast his vote for whatever was necessary to maintain the constitution. He gave his voice for the immediate calling of a Consultation of all the Colonies to meet at San Felipe for the purpose of discussing the questions of the hour. The next day he and Gail and John P. Borden, who attended the dinner with him, rode to San Felipe. The State government in Coahuila was overthrown and Texas had no State government and Austin assumed the functions of *de facto* ruler of the Province during the next thirty days.

There was at this time a dashing, ambitious, loquacious young man by the name of James W. Fannin, Colonel Fannin as he called himself, who had recently come to Texas and who was very active with the War Party. He was a slave-trader, the natural son of a Georgia planter

The Bordens Go to War

and had at one time been a cadet at West Point. He brought a cargo of slaves to Texas and had only been able to dispose of part of them due to the unsettled condition of the country. Colonel Fannin's plantation was on Caney Creek between Brazoria and Matagorda and he was riding up and down in the country fraternizing with those who were willing to open hostilities on short notice.

General Martin Perfecto Cos, brother-in-law of Santa Anna, was Commander-in-Chief of the military forces in Coahuila and Texas and during the last several months had sent repeated orders to the local authorities at San Felipe for the arrest of William B. Travis, Frank W. Johnson and others who had been instrumental in defying Mexican authority, for the purpose of having them transported to Coahuila for trial. The local authorities under pressure from the home people had refused to issue these warrants. Before Austin left Mexico he had talked with Santa Anna and had urged him under no circumstances to send troops to Texas and had told him that he believed that the troubles in Texas could be solved peacefully and Mexican authority restored if no show of military force was made.

On the 18th of September news reached the Colonies that General Cos had landed troops at Copano below Bexar and was marching them on to San Antonio for the purpose of coming into the Colonies and executing the warrants for the wanted men.

Colonel Fannin first heard this news from his home down on Caney and was quick to broadcast it and urge an immediate outpouring of citizens to form a volunteer army and meet what he called an invasion.

Austin heard it at San Felipe and was equally positive that Cos' forces should be resisted.

It therefore happened in the middle of September that Colonel Fannin down on Caney Creek and Colonel Austin up at San Felipe simultaneously declared war on Mexico, at least declared their intentions to resist the military intrusion of General Cos.

Volunteer soldiers from the Colonies were concentrating at Gonzales, sixty miles from San Antonio, and Austin planned going there at once to join the army, and it was necessary to establish some central authority to function until the consultation should meet a month hence. He chose a Committee of five persons selected from different municipalities to serve as a federal authority and a kind of clearing house for revolutionary activities during his absence. Gail Borden was selected as the member of this Committee from the jurisdiction of San Felipe. This Committee of five met at once and selected Richard Royster Royall of Matagorda to preside and began and continued its functions as the chief governmental instrumen-

The Bordens Go to War

tality of Texas until the Consultation met and organized in November.

These details arranged, Austin rode out of San Felipe on the 8th of October and joined the volunteer army that had gathered at Gonzales for the purpose of marching on to San Antonio and resisting General Cos.

On the same day that Austin left San Felipe the Bordens and Don Jose Baker issued No. 1, Volume 1 of the Texas Telegraph and Register. It was a modest sheet and contained little editorial matter, some current news and much war news. It was the only paper published regularly during the remainder of the year and when the Consultation met a few weeks later, it became and remained the official organ of the *de facto* government. On its press were published the circulars and broadsides which were carried here and there throughout the State, the doings of the Committee of which Gail Borden was a member, and the doings of the Consultation and the ad interim government which was organized by the Consultation. It reached all parts of the Colonies and performed those useful functions that in all such emergencies can only be performed by a newspaper.

The war spirit ran high along the coast where Captain James Collinsworth raised a company of thirty odd men and immediately took the road to Goliad for the purpose of intercepting General Cos. These Minute Men, farmers and herdsmen, hurried to Victoria where they tarried an hour and gathered recruits. Young John P. Borden was one of them. There was a Mexican population at Victoria and at Goliad to which place Captain Collinsworth's men were marching, and anxious to allay the fears of their Mexican fellow citizens they drew a formal declaration of fealty to the Mexican constitution of 1824 for which they declared they were fighting—a declaration that they intended to respect the rights and property of all citizens at Victoria and Goliad and signed it, pledging their sacred honor to its faithful observance.

This done, Collinsworth's men galloped off down the age-old road from Victoria to Goliad. Over this highway soldiers, priests and smugglers had traveled backward and forward for a hundred years. The Mexican fortress at Goliad had been a presidio since about 1749, established there to protect two missions that had been built among the Indians before the middle of the Seventeenth Century. During all the intervening years a small garrison of Spanish and Mexican soldiers had been maintained there, and around the presidio had grown up a small squalid village and there were ranches up and down the San Antonio River. A thousand Mexican people, more or less, lived at Goliad and in the vicinity.

At midnight on the 9th of October, Captain

The Bordens Go to War

Collinsworth with his Bay Prairie and Caney volunteers, rode stealthily into the town and rushed the fortress. They succeeded in capturing it without the loss of a single man and among the first to enter was John P. Borden.

In the meantime Colonel Austin had reached Gonzales where about three hundred volunteers had gathered and after a small skirmish with Mexican soldiers from Bexar, the three hundred were organized into a force which was given the grandiloquent name of the Federal Army and Colonel Austin was elected the Commander-in-Chief, and it took up the march to Bexar to oust General Cos. Paschal P. Borden was with Austin's army.

All four of the Bordens were now in active service, two of them on the firing line and the other two at San Felipe operating the press and supporting the *de facto* government.

The Federal army soon reached San Antonio but it was so poorly equipped that it made no immediate effort to capture the city, but invested and began a two months siege.

In the meantime John P. Borden, weary of idleness at Goliad, obtained leave to proceed to San Antonio and join Austin's army. One of the volunteers with this army long afterwards wrote a description of it which is interesting, even though ludicrous. "Words are inadequate (he says) to describe the appearance of the first Texas army. Nothing short of seeing it could do it justice. Buckskin breeches were the nearest approach to uniforms and there was wide diversity even there, some being new, soft and yellow, while others from long familiarity with the rain and grease had become hard, black and shiny; some from the process of wetting and drying on the wearer had reached a shortness exposing the shins guiltless of socks. Boots were an unknown quantity; some wore shoes and some moccasins. Here a broad brimmed sombrero overshadowed the military cap at its side and there a tall begum hat rode beside a coonskin cap with the tail hanging down behind as all well regulated tails should do. Here a big American horse loomed up beside a little Spanish pony; there a half-broke mustang pranced along beside a methodical mule. Here a roll of bed quilts jostled a pair of store blankets; there the shaggy brown buffalo robe contrasted with the gaily checkered counterpane on which the manufacturer had lavished all skill of dye and weave—mayhap it was part of the dowry of a wife brought her husband on her wedding day, and surely the day dreams she wove into its ample folds held in them no shadow of a presentiment that it might be his winding sheet. In lieu of a canteen each soldier carried a Spanish gourd. So with the old cannon flag flying at the head and the artillery flying at the heels of two yokes of oxen we filed out of Gonzales and took up our march to Bexar."

The Bordens Go to War

Colonel Austin was without military experience and most of the time was ill, often so ill that he could not sit on his horse. The siege lagged, some of the soldiers went home, others took their places, and as the autumn waned there was much discouragement in the army and back at home as well.

In November the Consultation, the convention of delegates from all the Colonies, met at San Felipe and organized. It chose a Governor, a Lieutenant Governor and a permanent Council which took the place of the Committee upon which Richard Royster Royall and Gail Borden had been sitting. This permanent Council composed of one delegate from each municipality soon proved an inefficient and unyieldy body and because of internal strife accomplished little to further the Patriot cause.

Early in December, the investing army at Bexar stormed and captured the City and General Cos and his entire force surrendered and were paroled and permitted to recross the Rio Grande.

John P., Thomas H. and Paschal P. Borden were all at the storming of Bexar and Gail Borden at San Felipe issued the edition of the Telegraph and Register which told the news of this momentus event.

At the end of the year there were no Mexican soldiers in Texas and many thought that the war was over, and most of the soldiers went home.

When the Consultation met in November the general sentiment seemed to be against a declaration of independence. It was confidently believed by many of the leaders in Texas, including Austin, that there was an influence in Mexico against the encroachment of Santa Anna that would join with the people of Texas in maintaining constitutional government. It was therefore decided that instead of declaring Texas an independent nation, that the Convention would merely declare its fealty to the Mexican constitution of 1824 and invite all those who held similar views in Mexico to join in resisting the encroachments of the Dictator. While there was a minority in this Convention that had no faith in aid from Mexico and favored immediate declaration of independence, yet the wiser course seemed a bona fide effort to maintain constitutional government without breaking the ties between Texas and the mother country. Austin felt a deep gratitude toward Mexico. The Colonists generally were mindful that during the last fifteen years it had been bountiful to them. The Bordens shared Austin's views in this as in other matters and the Bordens' paper during the entire autumn of 1835 spoke boldly for the restoration of the Mexican constitution.

Sam Houston had now come to Texas to

The Bordens Go to War

live and appeared at the Consultation as a delegate from Nacogdoches. He was elected Commander-in-Chief of the armies of Texas but Texas had no armies to command except the little three hundred that had been investing Bexar, under General Austin, and Houston's commission did not authorize him to displace Austin. For the time being Houston shared the views of Austin and the Bordens and those who thought it would be premature to make a declaration of independence until all efforts were exhausted to arouse a sentiment in Mexico that would co-operate with Texas.

General Santa Anna had long planned this coup by which he was to overthrow the constitution and make himself a Dictator and perhaps a King and he had planned it well. One by one the Mexican States had either through his manipulation or under the force of his military, submitted to his plan, and at the end of the year 1835 all of the States except Coahuila and Texas and some portions of other northern border States had expressed a willingness for a new order of things—a centralism by which the States would be reduced to departments and the Mexican confederation controlled by a central authority in the City of Mexico.

He shrewdly gave out the statement throughout Mexico that the entire country except the foreign element in Texas was agreeable to his plan, that these people were bent on separation from Mexico and that it was a patriotic duty for all Mexicans to rally and suppress these foreigners who had come into the country to rob the Mexican nation of one of its fairest provinces. He adroitly created the atmosphere of a foreign war and immediately began preparations for an invasion of Texas. At this time he was forty-four years old, had been in the army for more than thirty years, was a man of insinuating address and pleasing personality. And while he had few of the elements of a great commander he was indeed a great executive and organized an army of more than six thousand men and marched it as far north as Saltillo and at the beginning of the new year was ready to cross the river into Texas. Rumors of his contemplated invasion were being daily received in Texas and at the end of the year it was well known that a large and reasonably well disciplined army would soon cross the Rio Grande

Every issue of the Borden paper carried warnings of this imminent invasion and all during the autumn and winter Gail Borden was on the watch tower.

In this emergency the people of Texas feeling unequal to the contest began frantic appeals to their friends in the United States for aid. All during the autumn of 1835 soldiers had been coming into Texas from the Southern States, sometimes singly and in groups and in a few instances in organized companies. All through the

The Bordens Go to War

Southern States and as far north as Cincinnati mass meetings were being held by friends of Texas, money was being subscribed for the Texas cause, companies of soldiers were being equipped and were on the way to Texas.

Conscious of the fact that aid was coming from the States, the Mexican nation passed a decree in the autumn of 1835 that since it was at peace with the United States, that armed expeditions of soldiers coming from there into Mexico would be regarded as pirates and punished with death. Although this decree was widely published and well known it did not retard the constant flow of volunteer soldiers coming across the border, and in January, 1836 four-fifths of the men under arms in Texas were those recently arrived volunteers from the States.

Chapter VIII

THE BORDENS STILL AT WAR

The lull of the holiday season deceived no one in Texas who was willing to know the truth. At the dawn of the year it was known that General Santa Anna was at Saltillo ready to make an immediate descent on Texas.

Three of the Bordens had been at the siege at Bexar and they had returned home as most of the Texans had done after the capitulation of that place in December. The volunteer soldiers who had come into the State to take part in the campaign against Bexar and who had no homes to go to were wandering about aimlessly, some of them urging an immediate descent upon Matamoros, others remaining at San Antonio. Other volunteers were coming into the State and as early as January 1st there were three hundred Georgia and Alabama troops at the mouth of the Brazos ready to take part in the war. Colonel Fannin, who was a Georgian, had a commission from the *de facto* government at San Felipe which authorized him to take the command of these troops, and he took them down the coast to Copano and marched them to Goliad. One Francis White Johnson, who had been with the army at Bexar when it was captured, claimed the right to command the volunteer soldiers there and he took them down toward Matamoros, promising them an immediate descent upon the Mexican seaport town.

In the meantime General Houston, the Commander-in-Chief, still had no army to command and Colonel Fannin and Colonel Johnson were exercising commands entirely independent of each other and of him.

Foreseeing disaster from this chaotic situation Henry Smith, the Governor of Texas who presided at San Felipe, urged the Council which was exercising both executive and legislative functions, to co-ordinate the command of the

Texas forces and to avoid the disaster that must follow these independent movements. This resulted in a quarrel between him and the Council in which he was impeached in January. The Council was soon without a quorum and Texas without a government during January and February of 1836.

In the meantime, however, the Bordens continued their paper at San Felipe and kept the world advised as to what was going on.

In the latter days of February General Santa Anna with some two thousand men reached San Antonio. Colonel Travis, who had assumed command of such of the volunteers as remained there, was in the Alamo with about eighty men. It was the old mission fortress San Antonio Valero which had been established on the banks of the San Antonio River by the first Spanish Governor Alarcon in 1718. Adjoining it was the Presidio San Antonio founded in the same year and maintained continuously for one hundred and eighteen years as a Spanish garrison. Just below it was the Villa San Fernando de Bexar begun by the Canary Island immigrants in 1731 which for more than a century had been the only continuous civil settlement in Texas. Across the river a few miles below was the chain of deserted missions where many long vanished Indian tribes had faded away under the wasting influences of the white man's ways. The name Alamo came from the

The Bordens Still at War

cottonwood trees which grew about it. Adjoining the chapel was a stone wall enclosure of about a city block—such fortifications being an essential part of all the frontier missions. Here in the cloister many weary Franciscan priests had knelt in prayer as they passed on pilgrimages from Mexico to the Eastern missions. From its watchtower generations of padres had scanned the horizon to detect the ever-threatening approach of Apaches and Comanches, and had seen in the distance the signal smokes of the red warriors. Its broken walls were to become a sepulcher for many men of alien races who fought for the mastery of an empire.

The Mexicans besieged the Alamo for nearly three weeks when it was finally captured by an assault on the morning of March 6, 1836, and all the defenders slain. While this was going on General Santa Anna had sent his General Urrea up the coast by Matamoros to look after Fannin's men and Johnson's men and those straggling soldiers down that way who were planning a descent on Matamoros.

On March 2nd a Convention of delegates from the various municipalities of Texas met at Washington on the Brazos for the purpose of organizing a government and taking up the unfinished work of the late Consultation. Everyone now knew that there was no hope of aid from friendly influences in Mexico and that it was war to the death between the Texans and Mexico, so on this date the delegates declared the independence of Texas and immediately organized a *de facto* government, drew a constitution, elected a President and Vice-President and again chose General Houston Commander-in-Chief of the armies of Texas. But he was still without an army. The little garrison at the Alamo had been annihilated. Almost all the other armed forces in Texas were those with Fannin and Johnson in the southwest and General Urrea was moving on them with a well organized force.

On the morning of the 6th of March at about the same hour that the Alamo fell, Sam Houston rode out of Washington on the Brazos toward Bexar accompanied by two men and a boy. As he later said, with this equipment he was sent to defend a people and produce a nation. He reached Gonzales on the Guadalupe on the 11th of March where he found about three hundred men awaiting his coming. Shortly after his arrival news of the fall of the Alamo reached them, and the three hundred began an immediate retreat to the Colorado.

Among the companies recruited in the Colonies in this emergency was one of forty odd men raised by Captain Mosely Baker at San Felipe, and Paschal and John P. Borden and Moses Lapham marched out with this Company and it reached Gonzales before the retreat

The Bordens Still at War

began. Gail Borden enlisted with his brothers in Captain Baker's company but it was decided that he should stay with the printing press.

The ladies of San Felipe made a flag for the home boys and as Baker's men were ready to march, Gail Borden presented it with a stirring patriotic address.

Moses Lapham was on picket duty across the Guadalupe and when Houston's army left Gonzales in a mad rush he was forgotten and after an all day lonely vigil learned he had been abandoned and made haste to overtake his retreating comrades.

When the Patriot army reached the Colorado it had about a thousand men and was being followed by General Sesma, one of Santa Anna's Generals, with a force of about the same size. These armies camped on opposite banks of the Colorado River within firing distance of each other in the latter days of March.

In the meantime General Urrea coming up the coast had fallen on Johnson's men and annihilated them, after which he captured Fannin's entire command, which though it surrendered with a promise of treatment as prisoners of war, was on Palm Sunday, March 27th, stood before a firing squad and all were put to death except a small handful who escaped and a dozen or more who were spared for services they might perform for their captors.

News of the fall of the Alamo had hurried

Houston's army from the Guadalupe on March 11th and news of the massacre of Fannin and his men now hurried it from the Colorado. It was thirty miles from the camp on the Colorado to San Felipe on the Brazos and Houston's disorganized and bedraggled force of a thousand men came pouring into little San Felipe with word that the enemy was coming.

The great Commander stopped at San Felipe only a day, and after a quarrel with Captain Mosely Baker, who wanted to make a stand and fight, the General ordered a retreat up the river. Captain Baker refused to follow him and took his company across the river where it dug in the sand dunes and prepared to defend the crossing when the Mexicans should arrive. The two Bordens were still with Mosely Baker's men.

At this time there were thousands of people at the ferries on the Brazos, fugitives running away and the wildest excitement prevailed at San Felipe where General Santa Anna was daily expected.

Gail Borden had sent his family down to Fort Bend or the Fort Settlement, to the home of his brother Thomas H. Borden, and Thomas H. went with them to look after the safety of both families, while Gail was to undertake to get away with the press and prevent its falling into the hands of the enemy.

The ad interim government formed at

The Bordens Still at War

Washington on the Brazos a week before, headed by President Burnet, hurried away by the reports of the approaching enemy, had gone to Harrisburg on Buffalo Bayou about seventy miles below and was temporarily quartered there.

All Texas was on the run and every home west of the Brazos was deserted and the fleeing families were making frantic efforts to reach the Louisiana border. Tom Borden reached home on the last day of March and took his and Gail's families down the river to Velasco where a week later they crossed over to Galveston Island.

San Felipe was deserted and then burned, and Gail Borden and Don Jose Baker were left alone with their printing press. In this emergency he addressed a letter to President Burnet and dispatched it to Harrisburg fifty miles away. "Our army has retreated from the Colorado and it is necessary for us to remove our press. I shall endeavor to put it over the river today. If the government can send a team for it we will set it up at Harrisburg. It will require a large wagon and team. I have none. I send Mr. McGruder to inform you. If no team comes I must be in the bottom. Our army consists of upwards of a thousand men. Yours faithfully, Gail Borden, Jr."

The last issue of the Telegraph and Register published at San Felipe was under the date of

March 24th. Sometime in the latter part of that week Gail Borden and Joseph Baker managed to get their press transferred across the river at the San Felipe ferry.

The river was overflowing on the east bank and the press had to be placed on a raft and carried three miles over an inundated river bottom where it was dumped on the edge of a prairie where the proprietors of the Telegraph and Register were left stranded and desolate. John P. Borden, who had helped load the press on the ferry-boat and the raft, was with Captain Baker's company camped under the cottonwood trees on the east bank of the river within gun-shot of deserted San Felipe, and he found time from his military duties to seek out the marooned fugitives across the bottom who were keeping lonely vigil over their stranded outfit. President Burnet had not sent a wagon. Perhaps he had not gotten the message or more likely had no wagon to send. So John P. was sent all the way to Egypt on the Colorado for Eli Mercer's wagon and team and after a week of waiting it arrived and the precious press was loaded and they took off across the water-soaked prairies for Harrisburg at a pace of ten miles per day. The wagon was so heavily laden and the roads so bad that Borden and Baker had to walk all the way to lighten the load and almost hourly the vehicle would be bogged down and they would have to prize it out and put their

The Bordens Still at War

tired shoulders to the wheel to aid the horses. After a long muddy week during which it alternately rained and a norther blew, they plodded on, reaching Harrisburg on April 12th.

In the meantime General Santa Anna riding fast into the heart of the Colonies had reached San Felipe and finding Houston's army up the river in the woods, made no effort to follow it. He professed to think that General Houston was running away and would never come back. With fifty mounted men and five hundred soldiers he turned south along the river, seeking a crossing for the purpose of going after the fugitive ad interim government which was now quartered at Harrisburg. The river was bankful from recent rains and a crossing was difficult.

While many of the families at the Fort Settlement had left, a number of them remained. They seemed to think that their location was so isolated that the Mexican invaders would not find them. Besides Captain Wiley Martin with forty-six very valiant soldiers was defending big Jesse Thompson's ferry and this gave some sense of security.

Through spies with whom General Santa Anna was in contact he had learned of the location of this ferry, that it was an available place to cross. At midnight on the 11th of April he was in the margin of the big bend with his fifty horsemen, five hundred foot-soldiers following wearily behind.

In order to execute a surprise on Captain Martin's men the President halted at 2 o'clock in the morning several miles from the ferry and commenced a march on foot, slipping stealthily along through the huisache for the purpose of surprising the enemy at the crossing before daylight. Day broke upon him, however, a quarter of a league from the ferry and frustrated his plans, and he placed his men in ambush. While waiting there old Cain, one of John Morton's slaves had left the Morton home on the east bank of the river and was on his way across the bend with a message for his master who was with Wiley Martin's men at the ferry. He had crossed the river in a rowboat which he hid in the weeds. He was suddenly confronted by no less persons than General-President Santa Anna and Colonel Almonte who jumped out of the grass and nabbed him. He was then and there in the presence of the most august personages he had ever encountered in his life. He was taken into custody and made to conduct them to the little rowboat in which he had crossed and they took it and by making several trips managed to land fifty soldiers on the east bank of the swollen river several miles below Thompson's ferry. Captain Martin hearing that the Mexicans were crossing below him, with all his forty-six defenders, abandoned the ferry, and during the day Santa Anna's army ransacked the Fort Settlement, destroyed Thomas H. Borden's home

The Bordens Still at War

and gin, carried away all his chattel effects and crossed over the river. He, with the two families and the old father, had gone down the river two days before.

General Santa Anna now decided to make a quick dash to Harrisburg only thirty miles away where he hoped to capture President Burnet and the members of the ad interim government and take them home as trophies of war. He did not anticipate any trouble from Houston's army, for the last he had heard of it was when it was above San Felipe in the woods and he believed, or pretended to believe, that it was still hiding from him. He was flushed with his great victories and felt himself irresistible.

About the same hour General Santa Anna left the Fort Settlement with his fifty mounted men and five hundred foot-soldiers, Gail Borden and Joseph Baker driving Eli Mercer's wagon and team, drove into Harrisburg, found a vacant house, unlimbered their press and were ready for business. People were leaving, many of them already gone.

The first thing the firm of Baker & Borden did that day was to dissolve, and an announcement of that fact was inserted on the front page of the paper. "Don Jose" left at once in search of Houston's army and joined it and fought at San Jacinto a week later.

Gail Borden and his printer went to work to get out an edition of the paper under the dateline April 14th. The last heard of the Mexican army was somewhere west of the Brazos and he did not expect it at Harrisburg at least for the present. After an apology for the non-appearance of the paper since March 24th, he opened with this salutation: "We promise the public of our beloved country that our press will never cease its operation until our silence shall announce to them that there is no more in Texas a resting place for a free press nor for a government of the people." After this he gave the latest military news, including the account of the fall of the Alamo and such military orders as had been issued since the March 24th number.

While in the midst of the completion of the April 14th issue a runner warned that the Mexicans were approaching Harrisburg. Borden had but an hour in which to escape, and when General Santa Anna entered the town he found one of the printers still at the shop. The press was thrown in the river and the building was destroyed, but Borden carried away with him a few copies of the unfinished paper and some of them are still in existence. Thus ended for the time being the first efforts of the Bordens in journalism, and Texas was without a press for the next ninety days.

Gail Borden, along with President Burnet and other fugitives found his way to Galveston where he was met by Thomas H. Borden and

The Bordens Still at War

their families, they having come by way of the mouth of the Brazos.

General Santa Anna finding no one to oppose him at Harrisburg marched on down to the mouth of the bayou and camped on Galveston Bay, one of the margins of his vast empire which reached from Yucatan to Oregon, and from the Sabine to the Pacific. He seemed to think the war was over and contemplated a return home in triumph. In the meantime Urrea's victorious army was sweeping up the coast country and had reached the lower Brazos and was about to cross the bay to Galveston, while Filisola and Sesma with more than three thousand men were camped on the Brazos awaiting orders from El Presidente.

About the same time that Santa Anna was crossing the river at Thompson's ferry in the big bend and that Gail Borden and Joseph Baker reached Harrisburg, General Houston, whose army was hidden in the bottoms sixty miles above, crossed by means of a steamboat which had come up to the Groce plantation for cotton, and took up the march eastward. Just where he was going at this juncture he probably did not know, and certainly no one in the army knew. He did not know where Santa Anna was, he only knew that he had been to San Felipe and had marched down the river and had probably gone to join Urrea. Houston's plan since he had left Gonzales was to retreat and lure the enemy farther and farther into Texas. He had hoped for large reinforcements from the Red Lands, as the country in remote East Texas was called, that had not come. He confidently believed that if he could lead his army into the Red Lands that he would have further recruits and he probably expected aid from the United States troops on the border if he could get his army near the Sabine. There has always been a story that he had an understanding with President Jackson to lure Santa Anna to the border and that General Gaines, who was on the Sabine in command of United States troops, would find some way to help him.

On the third day after Houston had crossed the Brazos, able to move only a few miles a day due to the terrible condition of the roads, he reached a point called the Forks of the Road, a place where the road from San Felipe on the Brazos went north and eastward to Robbin's ferry on the Trinity, and on into the Red Lands, and where it was crossed by the road from Washington on the Brazos to Harrisburg. The left fork would take him east across the Trinity and on toward Nacogdoches, and the right fork to Harrisburg. There had been almost a mutiny in the army because of his failure to stand and fight, but he had taken no one into his confidence and rode grimly on.

While the army was camped above San Felipe it was rumored that certain malcontents

The Bordens Still at War

were about to beat-up for volunteers who would elect a commander to displace Houston, and he caused notices to be posted on the trees about the camp that the first one undertaking such an enterprise would be shot.

Here at the Forks of the Road a messenger came telling that Santa Anna had crossed the Brazos with only a few hundred men and had gone to Harrisburg. Whatever doubt may have existed as to Houston's intended movements before was dispelled now. Here was the chance for which he had been looking. Immediately the army took the right-hand road and marched toward Harrisburg. Mosely Baker had now rejoined the army, and Paschal P. and John P. Borden, Moses Lapham and Eli Mercer were in the ranks.

On the afternoon of the 19th of April with something less than a thousand men Houston's army crossed the bayou below Harrisburg and marched on down toward the bay, and on the early morning of the 20th camped in the woodlands near Lynchburg ferry about seven miles from the bay.

General Santa Anna was camped with his five hundred fifty men on the margin of the bay on the night of the 19th, and the morning of the 20th and was greatly surprised to hear that there was an armed force in his rear. He could go no farther south and immediately formed his troops in battle array and marched back towards the Lynchburg ferry. Sometime near noon on the morning of the 20th Houston's soldiers camped in the woodlands above the ferry, heard the strains of martial music borne by the soft south wind, and the armies were soon in sight of each other. Here they lay glaring at each other all during the remainder of the 20th and the morning of the 21st. Houston had almost twice as many men as Santa Anna but he hesitated to risk a battle with his raw recruits. On the morning of the 21st Santa Anna was reinforced by General Cos and now had between eleven and twelve hundred men.

Both armies had crossed Vince's bridge below Harrisburg as they came down and just after noon on the 21st General Houston sent Deaf Smith and Moses Lapham to destroy this bridge. At four o'clock in the April afternoon the Texans formed a thin battle line and charged the Mexican camp a mile away. As they reached the crest of the hill and were about to grapple the enemy, Deaf Smith and Moses Lapham came galloping among them brandishing their axes and telling that Vince's bridge had been destroyed. In fifteen minutes the Mexican army was routed, Santa Anna had fled with his fifty horsemen and when they reached Vince's bayou and found the bridge gone, he abandoned his horse and took to the woods and was captured the next day.

Chapter IX

THE BORDENS RETURN HOME

Thousands of fugitive families beyond the Trinity slept in the cold moonlight haunted by the bloody specters of Fannin's men and the Alamo. Every home from the Guadalupe to the Trinity was abandoned, and many soldiers who were at San Jacinto had loved ones somewhere among the fugitives. The forlorn mother with her dying babe on the Trinity or the Sabine prayed for an avenging hand, for deliverance, and had the Great Unseen smitten the enemy deliverance would not have been more swift and certain than that which followed. The vengeance of the Lord which smote the army of Sennecherib "when the Assyrians came down like a wolf on the fold," was not more deadly than the blow which had fallen on the invading army.

The night which followed the battle was that of a full moon in April and the battlefield and bayshore were flooded with its magic light, but all along the hillslope and across the Widow McCormick's field and down in the valley behind his Excellency's camp there were the motionless forms of the ghastly dead. The night was hideous with the agonies of the wounded and the piteous wails of the dying, while in the woodlands and down on the bayshore and prairies to the south came the weird howl of wolves who scented blood. All through the night and the days following, messengers were riding with the tidings, husbands and fathers were hurrying to find their families and bring them back. A horseman would ride up to a forlorn caravan of fugitives and tell the glad tidings too good to believe and hurry on scattering the news.

Nearly a week later one of these messengers rode into General Gaines' camp on the Sabine bearing a note written on a scrap of paper in

The Bordens Return Home

lead pencil and signed by Sam Houston telling of the victory in a single sentence. General Gaines called a young Lieutenant, Ethan Allen Hitchcock, a grandson of Ethan Allen of Ticondaroga, and dispatched him posthaste to Washington to deliver the terse memorandum to Andrew Jackson, President of the United States. Three weeks later after riding day and night the messenger bearing the most momentous news since the battle of Waterloo gave Houston's note to the President.

There were more than a thousand of these forlorn fugitives on Galveston Island. Hundreds of families from the lower Colorado and the Brazos who had crossed the bay at San Luis Pass were camped there. Others had been brought by boat down Buffalo Bayou and the Trinity. At that time there were only five or six houses on the Island and all of these homeless fugitives were camping in the open. Most of them had brought few of their belongings and were without tents for shelter.

The ad interim President of the Republic and his Cabinet were there; Gail and Thomas H. Borden and their families were there. Gail Borden's family at that time consisted of his wife, Penelope, the oldest daughter, Mary, who was born on Galveston Island a few hours after the family landed there the first time in 1829, the oldest son, Henry Lee, who was born at Egypt on the Colorado in 1832 and the baby, Morton

Quinn, born in 1834. Thomas H. Borden's family consisted of his wife, who was Demis Woodward, and two little boys, two and five years old. Their old father, Gail Borden, Sr., was with them.

None of the refugees had heard any news from the mainland for several days. Even the latest comers to the Island did not know where General Houston's army was. President Burnet had tried to get in contact with it before he left the mainland four days previously but had been unable to locate it. They all knew that Santa Anna's army had come as far as Harrisburg and that some of his soldiers had been seen at Morgan's Point. Burnet had seen them riding down the hill as he pushed off from old Morgan's warehouse—landing in a rowboat. They had rumors that Urrea's army which had crossed the Brazos was near the west end of Galveston Island and might cross over and attack the refugees. In fact this was Urrea's plan when he heard of the news of the battle of San Jacinto.

There were no boats in the harbor that could take the refugees anywhere, and there seemed nowhere for them to go. And so these thousand fugitives lived from day to day with apprehension and in the greatest despair.

Although it was late in April, the nights were cold and the week before a severe norther had blown which had sent a deadly chill throughout the entire population. Measles had broken out among them, the old and decrepit were dying and children were born on this barren beach.

On Monday morning, April 25th, watchers on the north beach saw a rowboat coming across the bay from the mainland from what is now called Virginia Point. Its movements were slow and one man seemed to be rowing while the other was bailing water. It bore messengers from General Houston and General Rusk to President Burnet with official information of the battle of San Jacinto. Benjamin C. Franklin and Robert J. Calder, two young men who had fought as privates in that battle and had been dispatched with these messages three days before, were making their way from the San Jacinto battlefield, a distance of about seventy miles, in a leaky rowboat.

When the boat landed, the messengers were immediately surrounded by an eager throng and without waiting to deliver their official communication to the President broadcast the news of the victory. At first the people could not believe it. It seemed utterly incredible, but the well known reputation of the messengers and the official communication they bore soon convinced the wary islanders that deliverance had come.

The refugees were kept from starvation by a timely distribution of food from one of the boats from New Orleans bearing military supplies for the army.

When General Santa Anna was brought into the Texas camp a prisoner the day after the battle he readily agreed to an armistice and that the Mexican army which was then on and west of the Brazos should retire beyond the Rio Grande, and he sent messengers to General Filisola and General Urrea to carry these instructions into effect. And with their more than five thousand men they began a retreat which soon amounted to a rout and within sixty days the last of the invading army had recrossed the river. There were, however, rumors of a new invasion and the Texas army was kept under arms for nearly a year on account of these recurring rumors.

Paschal, John P. Borden and Moses Lapham for the time being remained with the Texas army. All the while the fugitives were returning. The thousands who had crossed the rivers going toward the Louisiana border were coming back, seeking the ferries and other available crossings and many of them came back the Lynchburg way which brought them across the San Jacinto battlefield.

Nearly a week after the battle William Stafford, a Fort Bend planter, came driving home with his wife and children. They found the Mexican dead strewn all along the highway for no one had taken the pains to bury them,

The Bordens Return Home

and they drove far enough to evade the stench and camped for the night on the prairie.

Paschal Pavalo Borden, who was probably hunting congenial company, wandered from his army camp that evening and visited with the Stafford family. Stafford's daughter Martha was then sixteen and an acquaintance began which resulted in the marriage of Paschal Pavalo Borden and Martha Stafford a few years later.

All the while the families on Galveston Island were gradually gathering themselves together and making their exit. Thomas and Gail Borden were without means of transportation. They foregathered with other fugitives from up the Brazos and procured a boat in which they crowded their families, and in the early days of May the two families landed at the Fort Settlement at Big Bend at the home of Thomas H. Borden.

It would be hard to visualize a more desolate place than they found on their homecoming. The houses had been burned and every article of personal property and furnishings and every useful thing had been taken from the farm, and the gin had been burned. It was like beginning life anew when they all sat down for a family conference to take into consideration the state of their fallen fortunes.

General Houston had been wounded at San Jacinto and it became necessary for him to go to New Orleans for treatment, and the command of the army had been delivered to Rusk who was following the retreating Mexican army. Rusk's army reached the Brazos early in May and camped there for a few days.

There was a family conference of the Bordens up at Thomas H. Borden's camp in the Bend. The old father, his four sons and the little families of Thomas H. and Gail were present. It was too late for them to plant a crop and harvest anything for the current year except corn. Their money was all gone, provisions were scarce and it seemed to require almost a miracle to prevent starvation. Their printing press was at the bottom of the bayou. Even their surveying instruments were lost. But they were young and full of determination and hope. Gail Borden, Jr. was now in his thirty-sixth year, and John P., the youngest, was twenty-four. They made ambitious plans at this May meeting—they would all resume their surveying work just as soon as they could get together the necessary equipment. They knew that there would be much demand for these services in the next few months, for immigrants would be coming into Texas and lands would be in demand. They would open a land office and become land agents, and Thomas H. and Gail Borden determined to revive their defunct press. It did not occur to them to go back to the bayou and undertake to find the one that had been thrown into the water although this

The Bordens Return Home

was done some years later and a paper was published on it. They had evidences of indebtedness from the ad interim San Felipe government amounting to about $7,000 for printing they had done during the last five months, but there was no money in the treasury and they could not realize any cash on this collateral. It was decided that Paschal P. and John P. would remain with the army for the time being and Thomas would plant a corn crop and that Gail would undertake to get some employment with the ad interim government, and as soon as they could arrange details that one or both of the older brothers would go somewhere and buy a new printing press. With the same persistent courage that had characterized their lives before and that was manifest in the life of Gail Borden to the end, they went to work to retrieve their fallen fortunes.

President Burnet and his Cabinet bringing the captive President of Mexico along, took up headquarters for the time being at the little town of Velasco at the mouth of the Brazos. The army moved on west following the retreat of Filisola and Urrea and camped on the Guadalupe.

As soon as Tom Borden planted his corn crop he started out for the States for the purpose of purchasing a new printing outfit. He first went to New Orleans but unable to make a purchase there took a river steamer for Cincinnati where after long negotiations he succeeded in raising enough money with the government warrants and such land as he and his brother owned, to enable them to buy a new press. Sixty days later he was back on the Brazos with it and in the first week of August following, Gail and Thomas H. Borden, proprietors and publishers, issued Vol. 1, No. 23 of the Telegraph and Register. It bore the simple slogan, "We go for our country."

The first page of Vol. 1, No. 23, was devoted to the publication of the constitution of the Republic of Texas that had been adopted at the Convention in March but which had never been published in Texas until this time. The original had been hurriedly taken away by the Secretary of the Convention, who fled to the United States, and was published in a Nashville, Tennessee, paper in June and republished in a Cincinnati paper in July and when Thomas H. Borden was in Cincinnati he had procured a copy of this Cincinnati paper containing the constitution and brought it back with him and it served as the official copy, the original having been lost and never recovered.

On the second page of the August 2nd paper they made modest reference to their new venture. "Our paper again makes its appearance under circumstances more auspicious than the suspension of its publication was discouraging. The cause of Texas has not expired with the

The Bordens Return Home

destruction of our press but that cause is now completely triumphant, and our independence won by valor which it is hoped wisdom will secure. We have engaged the principal portions of our property in its re-establishment. Nevertheless we shall consider ourselves amply repaid if we can win the confidence of the people and have their patronage. It has now been three and a half months since our last issue No. 22, the 14th of April was published."

They then recount the experiences that attended the removal from San Felipe to Harrisburg and tell of the ravages that the invading army had wrought at their home in Fort Bend. "Although stripped of every vestige of personal property we wish to continue the publication of our paper and especially is this true since the government has requested it. Notwithstanding all these embarrassments and difficulties we announce to the citizens of Texas that we are ready to go forward and furnish them with the press and we are ready once more to defend the cause of the country. Our slogan is, 'We go for our country,' and we will abstain from any partisan conflict and from inserting any articles dictated by private spite or malevolence."

They had brought their press to the little town of Columbia on the Brazos some thirty miles from the mouth of the river, for it had been determined that the first Congress of the Republic to be elected in September would meet there in October and that this for the time being would be the seat of the government for the Republic.

In the preceding July President Burnet had called an election for President, Vice-President, members of Congress and for the purpose of the submission of the constitution for ratification. An election campaign was on when the republication of the paper was begun, and being the only paper published in Texas its importance was manifest.

Stephen F. Austin was a candidate for President and, of course, had the support of the Bordens.

President Burnet and his Cabinet had negotiated a treaty between Texas and Mexico with General Santa Anna in the latter part of May, by the terms of which the independence of Texas was to be recognized by Mexico and the captive President was to be returned to his native country in order to carry out the provisions of the treaty. This procedure met violent opposition from many of the citizens and all of the Texas army, because they said that Santa Anna would not carry out the treaty and for the further reason he should be hanged for his high crimes and misdemeanors, especially for his having directed the massacre at Goliad. After the treaty was negotiated the captive President was placed on board a Texas man o' war at the mouth of the river and was about to be trans-

The Bordens Return Home

ported to Vera Cruz in keeping with its terms. Companies of volunteer soldiers that were coming to enlist in the Texas service were constantly arriving daily and one of these landed the very day that the Mexican President was to sail. These newcomers were not satisfied with President Burnet's treaty and at once took charge of the situation and went on board the "Invincible," forcibly removed Santa Anna and returned him to Velasco where he was held to await the disposition of the Congress that was to be chosen in the September election.

While Bordens' paper did not take any issue as to the disposal of Santa Anna, yet both the Bordens were heartily in favor of supporting the ad interim government.

No sooner had Austin announced for President than he was assailed from all corners with the usual malignant statements made against men seeking public office. He was charged with having been overfriendly to Mexico, with having at first opposed the independence of Texas, and worse than all, with the participation in the land frauds in Coahuila by which 1100 leagues of Texas land had been granted to speculators in 1835. This last charge grew out of the fact that Samuel M. Williams, Secretary of his Colonies and long his partner, was a participant in these land transactions. Gail Borden, who knew the facts and who loved Austin dearly, addressed him an open letter and asked him to make a statement refuting it. "For," said Borden in his letter, "I will wager my life that you are entirely innocent." Austin did make a straightforward dignified statement, and it was published in Borden's paper. But on the eve of the election General Sam Houston returned from New Orleans, limping on crutches, suffering from a wound he had received at the battle of San Jacinto, and was announced as candidate for President and was overwhelmingly elected.

The first Congress of the Republic of Texas met as per schedule at Columbia on the Brazos in October, 1836, and the Bordens' paper continued through the entire session of the Congress to be the official organ of the government and the only paper published in Texas.

Again the Bordens accumulated large evidences of indebtedness from the bankrupt government which they were unable to collect for many months to come. In the meanwhile they had prepared themselves to do surveying work and under the name of Borden and Company, Thomas H. and Gail Borden and Moses Lapham were actively engaged through the entire autumn of 1836 and the year following in this work.

On the 30th of August of that year their paper contained an advertisement that certain promoters by the name of Allen had purchased a desirable tract on Buffalo Bayou above Harrisburg and were about to locate the city of

The Bordens Return Home

Houston which they predicted would be the metropolis of Texas and its Capital. To this day the people of Houston celebrate August 30th, the date of this publication, as the birthday of Houston and they celebrated its one hundredth birthday on August 30, 1936. The Allens employed Gail and Thomas H. Borden to make the preliminary survey and lay off the city of Houston, and Gail Borden and Moses Lapham came forthwith and engaged in the work and made the first official map of the city of Houston.

Moses Lapham while engaged in the work wrote to his father in Ohio that the site was not very healthy and that he had been attacked with chills and fever, and without medicine and had doctored himself by drinking great draughts of black pepper which brought on a prespiration and gave him relief.

At about the same time their services were enlisted for surveying the townsite for Galveston.

They tried city building on their own account. Several years before Thomas H. Borden had conceived the idea of a city of Louisville in the big bend of the Brazos. Other promoters now started a town below the bend which they called Richmond, but the Bordens, who owned land from the curve of the bend down to and contiguous to the Richmond townsite determined that they would locate a town and name it Bordentown and they made an ambitious survey and subdivision and advertised lots for sale in Bordentown.

In the autumn of 1836 Congress at Columbia was called upon to select a site for the Capital of Texas for the next three years with the thought that it would be somewhere upon or near the coast and ultimately would be removed farther inland as the country away from the coast was settled. Texas at the time of the Revolution consisted of the land from the Sabine to the Nueces south of the old Nacogdoches-San Antonio road, at no distance more than two hundred miles from the coast. All of the Anglo-American colonies were within this area and all the country north and west of this line was now (1836) wild Indian country, as savage as it had been when the Spaniards first came three hundred years before.

When the question of selection of a site for a temporary Capital was presented to Congress in December, Thomas H. Borden presented a memorial to that body urging his site in the big bend of the river as a most desirable one. But the promoters of the town of Houston seemed to have done a wise thing when they named their prospective city Houston, and on the third ballot it was selected as the Capital. Tom Borden's site getting only one vote.

Columbia, the temporary Capital, was a squalid little place of shacks which afforded

The Bordens Return Home

little comfort to the over-crowded population. Hundreds of persons, young and old, had become debilitated and ill from the exposures of the runaway scrape and the death rate at Columbia during the autumn and winter was appalling. Thomas H. Borden's young wife died there in September and he was left with their two beautiful little motherless boys. Moses Lapham, who wrote his folks back in Ohio of this melancholy event, described her as a woman of rare attainments. She was buried beneath the age-old oaks on the Bell plantation and ninety-nine years later her grandchildren removed her remains to Galveston where they rest beside her husband.

Two years after the war Thomas H. Borden had rebuilt his houses and his gin in the Big Bend and wrote Gail, still using the name "Louisville" to denote his location,—that he had ginned sixty-seven bales of cotton which would bring him out of debt. He was still having trouble with some of his neighbors. One of Big Jesse Thompson's sons had become Sheriff of the county and they still owned a plantation near him. Living in this atmosphere with his two little boys he was apprehensive. "Oh that I had never come here," he wrote. "There was an attempt to assassinate me on last Wednesday, but I cannot write you the particulars."

The first Congress of the Republic held its session at Columbia from October until December when it adjourned to meet at the newly selected Capital at Houston on Buffalo Bayou in the following May and the Bordens continued to publish their paper at Columbia until all departments of the government had vacated there, then they followed to Houston.

One of the first and most important problems which confronted the new Congress was the establishment of a land office and the centralization of the files and archives of the various empresarios who had maintained different offices during the entire Colonial period. More than 20,000,000 acres of land had been granted to persons now in Texas by the Mexican government and these titles were shown by records that were kept by the several empresarios all the way from the Nueces to Nacogdoches. The chief colonial grants had been to Austin, who had located four colonies. Austin's archives had been carefully kept at San Felipe under his supervision and with the aid of Samuel M. Williams and Gail Borden, who had from time to time assisted him.

Prior to the Revolution Austin had arranged with Gail Borden to make a comprehensive map of Texas which would properly plot all of his colonial grants but the work had not been finished when the war began. When the Mexican army was approaching San Felipe and Gail Borden was hurrying out with his press and everybody else was getting away as fast as he

The Bordens Return Home

could, one Dr. Peebles, who was for the time being in charge of Austin's office (Austin then being in the United States), loaded the entire archives of the Austin colonies on a wagon and took them to faraway Nacogdoches where they were kept until after the Revolution. They were now brought back to Columbia and taken to Austin's home at Peach Point and he arranged for Gail and John P. Borden to classify and index the records and complete the map and do everything necessary to having them perfected and turned over to the new government. This work was enormous and took several months of their time for which they were paid $2,500.

Late in December Congress passed an act creating a Land Office and providing for a Land Commissioner whose duty it would be to take charge of all of these archives and to see that they were arranged and preserved.

Those of the other Empresarios were widely scattered, some of them having been taken away by the Mexican army.

President Houston named young John P. Borden first Commissioner of the General Land Office and he took charge in 1837. His experience in working with the San Felipe archives, his knowledge of Spanish and his industry made the first Land Commissioner of Texas a most efficient one. He set to work to gather these archives and after more than a year succeeded in doing so, and organized a General Land Office along the lines it has been conducted to this day. Those familiar with the details unhesitatingly say that it is the best kept department of the State government and one of the best organized and operated offices in the world. The efficiency and honesty of the General Land Office of Texas from the time of John P. Borden until this day has been a by-word with the people of Texas.

Austin defeated for the office of President accepted the position of Secretary of State in the Cabinet of President Houston and went forward performing duties which his health forbade. Late in December he sickened and it was evident that he was on his death-bed. Gail Borden, who was living in Columbia at the time, was his constant attendant and when Austin died on the 27th of December, tall, gaunt, frail looking Gail Borden stood by, tears coursing down his cheeks. He loved Austin with a devotion which was not dimmed by the years, and Austin loved him. During the preceding month when there was so much talk of fraud in Texas, someone asked Austin, "Is there an honest man in Texas?" And Austin promptly replied, "Yes Gail Borden." He followed Austin to his grave and forty years later, in one of the last letters he ever wrote he paid a great tribute to the memory of the saintly Stephen F. Austin.

At the close of the year 1836 everything was in readiness for the removal of the Capital from

The Bordens Return Home

Columbia to Houston. The first advertisement of Houston was not made until the 30th of August and the map showing its streets and subdivisions was not published until October and the first house was not begun until December. But since Congress was to meet there the following May it was necessary to move with great celerity and its owners were busy cutting down the pine forests and preparing the foundations of the city.

The Telegraph and Register, still the only paper published in Texas, the official organ of the government, must, of course, follow the government, and the Bordens were face to face with the necessity of moving again. They were not, however, hurried out as they had been when they left San Felipe the preceding March or when they left Harrisburg on the 14th of April, but took their time. Their last issue in Columbia was printed on April 11, 1837, and it required them from that date until the 2nd of the following May to get established in Houston, though only sixty miles away.

On May 2, 1837, they published Vol. 2, No. 15, their first issue in the new town of Houston.

In this issue they apologized for the delay saying, "We left Columbia on the steamboat 'Yellowstone' on April 16th, but were delayed a week at the bar off Velasco. We were then stranded at Clopper's Bar for a day and reached Lynchburg on the 26th whence we proceeded at the rate of one mile an hour to the head of navigation at Houston on Buffalo Bayou."

Before leaving Columbia, however, Gail and Thomas H. Borden had dissolved their partnership in the paper. It had been arranged that President Houston would appoint Gail Borden Collector of the Port at Galveston, and he intended to move there. Thomas H. Borden retained his interest in the paper for a short while and disposed of it in the following year, but it continued to be run in Houston as the leading paper for nearly forty years.

Paschal and John P. Borden and Moses Lapham severed their connection with the army in the autumn of 1836. John P. became Commissioner of the Land Office, Paschal returned to his plantation, and Moses Lapham joined Thomas H. Borden in surveying work. In the following year they had a contract to do some land locating near San Antonio, and Lapham took his outfit and repaired to that place. In November, after he had gone, Paschal Pavalo Borden wrote Moses Lapham's father in Ohio: "Your son was killed near Bexar on the 20th by the Comanche Indians, being at that time on a surveying expedition, a business in which he had been engaged for about six months previous. The circumstances of his death, as I have just been informed by a letter from particular friends of mine, are as follows: The evening of the 20th they were on the Presidio-Rio Grande road

The Bordens Return Home

when they were overtaken by a band of hostile Comanches. Moses and the four men with him scattered and went into the bushes and had they remained there until night they might have escaped, but as it was, he was found the next day a considerable distance out in the open prairie with an arrow sticking in his body and scalped."

The firm of Bordens and Lapham was now dissolved, and Gail Borden was about to assume his duties as Collector of the Port at Galveston.

Chapter X

THE GAIL BORDENS GO TO GALVESTON

For the more than ten years Gail Borden had been in Texas his life had been one of continuous toil. Sometimes a farmer and herdsman, always a surveyor, going on exposed frontiers as far north as the Milam Colony, as far west as the Guadalupe, often exposed to danger from hostile Indians. Traveling on horseback and on

The Gail Bordens Go to Galveston

foot, exposed to heat and cold, he had come to look prematurely old at forty. He and Thomas H. had now sold the Telegraph and Register and he coveted an easier life than he had known during the last decade. All during these years, all his life in fact, he had fugitive notions in a vague way of inventions which came to him as in a dream, for his mind never rested and was in an eternal quest for some hidden truth, following some principle, some shadowy half-truth.

President Houston, who like Austin held him in high regard and dignified him as the soul of integrity, offered him the post of Collector of the Port of Galveston. The salary was small, barely enough for a living for his family, which now consisted of four small children—Henry Lee, the oldest son, then about six years old.

Galveston was indeed a primitive place, one hundred houses had been built in the last year on the east end of the Island, built hurriedly with lumber shipped in from sawmills up the coast and few of them had the adornment of paint. Box houses, California houses as these shells came to be called a few years later, often without ceilings and as often a single board for the wall without weatherboarding. Gail Borden often told that the first house he lived in on Galveston Island was built in half a day. Colonel Amasa Turner, who came the same year to become military commander of the port, said that he constructed for his family a room ten by eleven feet built of mere sod-grass taken from the bayshore by Mexican prisoners and cut in brick-shape with spades and thatched with the same grass. The Mexicans called it a "casa grande."

But the climate was wonderful and the gardens tropical, mild summer-like winters and gulf winds which blew all day and all the summer nights. The importance of the place as a port was becoming worldwide and the ships of all nations were coming and going and the little navy of the Republic sailed in and out of the harbor bringing prizes picked up in the Gulf, for Texas was still figuratively at war with Mexico. On one of its home-coming trips Admiral Moore brought ten thousand dollars in gold which had been earned on a cruise down Campeachy way.

The city had now been incorporated and that genial soldier of fortune, Captain John M. Allen, was its first Mayor. A Kentuckian, he had sailed as a midshipman on a United States man o' war many years before. When the vessel was in the Mediterranean he had taken leave and joined the Greek Revolutionists whose war for freedom against Turkey had aroused the world. Midshipman Allen had joined a regiment which included the great English poet and patriot, Lord Byron, and Captain Allen was with this renowned eccentric when he died at

The Gail Bordens Go to Galveston

Missolonghi in 1824. Having buried the poet and seen Greece free, his work in Attica was done.

Home again and penniless the Captain was in New Orleans in the autumn of 1835 when three companies of soldiers were being recruited for the aid of the Texas Revolution, and he joined one of them, the New Orleans Grays, and sailed for Tampico with General Jose Mexia. At Tampico half the company of Grays were captured and shot, but Captain Allen escaped with the remnant to Texas, joined the Patriot army and fought under General Houston at San Jacinto.

Now in his forties, one of the handsomest men in Texas, he, like Gail Borden, craved a more restful life and he became the first Mayor of the first port of Texas.

After Borden served as Collector for the Port he was retained as Executive Secretary for the Galveston City Company, the corporation that owned the Galveston townsite and was developing the city. His salary was small but sufficient for his immediate needs, and the employment was not irksome and afforded him much leisure. He maintained this connection for more than ten years.

At the conclusion of his term as Collector of the Port of Galveston a controversy arose between him and the Republic which grew out of the depreciated value of the currency in which he had accepted payments from importers as to whether he should be allowed to settle in this depreciated currency at its face or par value, or its depreciated value. He claimed the right to make the former settlement. His bondsmen were McKinney and Williams, who were large creditors of the government for supplies furnished during the Revolution for which they had never received payment. They had him turn over to them the currency he had received and undertook the defense of the suit and tendered their evidences of indebtedness in payment of the government's claim. There never was any question of misappropriation of money. It was merely, what kind of a settlement and in what kind of money he should make payment. The lawsuit worried him very much, for it was the only one he had ever experienced. Brother Huckins, who visited him during its pendency and when it was about to come to trial, tells that he heard him in his garden praying for divine aid in the controversy. But the necessities of the impoverished Republic were such that it could not afford to pay its debts at par to McKinney and Williams, nor could it accept its depreciated currency at par. While Brother Borden's prayers were not answered in this behalf, it did not in the least shake his simple faith in the power and necessity of prayer, though it may have done so in the integrity of his government.

The Gail Bordens Go to Galveston

What Gail Borden's ill-shaped box house lacked in beauty was well supplied with a tropical garden in which huge leafed banana plants grew in profusion, flowering vines covered its rough exterior, a fig orchard had matured in a single year and oleanders blossomed summer and winter.

All the pent-up mental energy of a lifetime now broke forth in his passion for research and invention and he had schemes all the way from condensed foods to a terraqueous machine in which he combined the idea of an automobile, a seaplane and an aeroplane. Days, nights and weeks he worked on this monstrosity in a closed "garage" to obscure his efforts from the heat of the sun and the curious town-folks. The wind was to be its motor power—those constant high trade-winds which blew forever across the sandy beach and howled in the gables of his shell of a home. Finally he assembled a queer looking cross between a wagon and a sailboat and invited a select party of his friends (everybody on the Island loved him), for a night ride along the beach under the soft radiance of the midsummer moon. There were misgivings but the confident inventor told them that it was safe as a farm wagon. First he assembled his guests at his home and served them a dinner. It was a strange menu of soups, condensed foods, extracts, more synthetic than natural. He alone seemed to enjoy the meal which afforded a medley of odd odors and flavors.

Mayor Allen was there; General Bates, the three hundred pound sugar and cotton planter who farmed from his Galveston home a plantation upon Oyster Creek, was there with his two daughters; the editor of the local paper; the new minister and others.

The terraqueous monster was pulled across the sand to the smooth beach by a team of horses which were as timid about it as the passenger-guests, and finally adjusted on the smooth beach. The passengers were seated inside, and the inventor at the throttle. The trade-wind tore away at its flapping sails and off it went down the beach five, ten miles an hour, and when it reached this breakneck speed some of the women guests began to scream, and there was a wild demand that he stop it. But he was outside and could not hear their screams until the whole passenger cabin became a riot predominated by hysterical women who were led in a loud chorus by the daughters of General Bates, all demanding that the infernal machine be stopped forthwith. In an effort to do so the conductor became involved and the terraqueous machine was turned into the surf, which was beating on the moonlit shore, was turned over and smashed up with no worse results to the passengers than a saltwater plunge from which

The Gail Bordens Go to Galveston

the women were gallantly rescued by the men present.

All the while the editor stood by and made notes by moonlight for the next issue of the weekly paper.

The young minister, who was much of the time a guest in Brother Borden's home, has left us an interesting glimpse of the inventor's environment during these first years of his effort in the vast field which ranged from mechanics to meat biscuit and condensed milk.

They walked through his fig orchard to a place where an enormous kettle was installed over a rude out-of-door furnace. "Here," the host told him, "I will put in water, half a hogshead of sugar, a cartload of figs, then heat, press, condense and preserve into ten-pound containers made strong for the purpose. The world is coming to the idea of concentration and condensing."

There was a small warehouse nearby where he had cans of condensed chicken and in one box or case of cans he pointed out, a calf, in another a drove of turkeys. He said some friends from down about Goliad had promised him a wargonload of terrapins and he was going to try out terrapin soup. There were pots, kettles and vats all about, and the good wife, Penelope, who shook her head and laughed at his inventions, showed the young minister a dining table with a stationary outer rim upon which the diner would place his plate while the table behind the rim on which the dishes and food were placed would revolve at the touch of a spring and keep the victuals passing before the guest and within easy reach. And good Gail Borden confided in his guest that his sole ambition in all this quest was to make money to be used in salvaging a wicked world, spreading the gospel, doing good.

In his early forties he was getting gray, was over six feet tall, very gaunt, with a kindly wistful face and without an enemy in the world. Born in the Baptist faith he had always accepted its dogmas as he understood them but had been too busy for many years to give much thought to other than making a living for his growing family. He had never wronged anyone and his conscience was as clear as his public record. All the world in which he moved accorded him the encomium which Austin had given him, "Gail Borden is an honest man." But in those days the orthodox Baptist preacher was quick to warn the layman that mere observance of the Golden Rule or any other high rule of conduct was not enough, that a man must be borne again, born of the water and the spirit, or he could not enter the kingdom of Heaven.

Serious, devout men of God were carrying the gospel along these lines into the frontier

The Gail Bordens Go to Galveston

places. Reverend Jesse Mercer had now made Georgia the greatest Baptist State and was reaching out for new worlds. He had made donations, large for that day, and now hearing of the new fertile field of Texas which the Revolution had snatched from the Pope's domain, he raised $2,500 and sent a missionary to Texas.

Reverend James Huckins was a huge broad-shouldered, leather-lunged man, with a voice which was only excelled by his zeal, and one of the first places he invaded was Galveston where he was soon at home with the Bordens. He held a revival and told his hearers of the awful peril which hung over the recalcitrant who had not repented and been baptized. The penalty was awful, a hell which was eternal, where self-replenishing fires burned forever and the dead who went without the essentials of salvation were burned and burned in this cauldron throughout eternity. A man could not lift himself into Heaven by his own deeds unaided by the Divine anymore than he could defy the laws of gravitation and lift himself by pulling on his own boot-straps. The self-righteous man who sought Heaven on his own momentum without repentance, rebirth and baptism was doomed, while the sinner who at the end of a long wicked life repented on his death-bed was saved. It all depended on the status of the soul at the time of departure.

All this and more Brother Huckins told them.

Neither Brother nor Sister Borden had given these things the consideration they deserved, nor had the real plight of the unredeemed been fully presented to them in its true light. Neither of them had any sins to confess, but nevertheless they were "convicted" and with contrite spirit knelt at the mourners bench while Brother Huckins lifted his stentorian voice to Heaven in their behalf. They were "converted" and must be baptized.

Brother Huckins in an earnest letter to his spiritual father, Jesse Mercer back in Georgia, told of the great triumph. "There was a Brother Gail Borden," he wrote, "whose wife is a granddaughter of the late Reverend Thomas Mercer. The Brother and his wife have loved the cause of Christ for years and have been waiting and praying for more than ten years for some servant of Christ of their own faith to come and preach to them the word of life and baptize them and I was the first to come. For five years they had not seen a minister of Christ or had the privilege of attending a religious meeting, but they have not spent these years of solitude and affliction in hunting and fishing on the Sabbath as many others have done. No, when they could not find a single individual to join them, they have spent their Sabbaths in reading the scripture and in prayer and they

The Gail Bordens Go to Galveston

have always held family prayers in their home. The ordinance of baptism took place on the south side of the island. The grandeur of the scenery conspired with the moral sublimity of the occasion to awaken the strongest and most thrilling emotions. On one side as far as the eye could see, lay the vast prairies, on the other the boundless expanse of old ocean lashing with its deep blue waters the very ground on which we stood, the ever rolling billows resembling the distant voice of God. There were with Gail Borden, his wife and her sister and her brother. I warned all present to prepare for the last great day . . . This was the first baptism in the Gulf of Mexico west of the Mississippi. There are other Baptists here and we will organize them into a church. Next Lord's day we will receive ten or twelve brethren of color."

Brother Huckins added at that time (1840) Galveston had 600 houses and 3000 people and that he was about to depart for Houston which was, so he had heard, very much in need of the gospel.

It is odd that the account of this lonely little baptismal ceremony nearly one hundred years ago should have been so well reported. A devout sister, who was present visiting from far away Virginia, wrote a circumstantial report to her brother in Richmond. She too was impressed with the occasion. "Brother Borden," she wrote, "stands high in the Republic for sterling integrity and high-toned morality. He and his lady had been waiting ten years to be baptized into the church and all during these years have been mercifully preserved throughout great dangers. Brother Borden was led into the water and immersed and Mrs. Borden and her sister were then buried with the Lord."

This detail was now settled and the Bordens, in whom blended the ancestry of Roger Williams and the Mercers, had made the irrevocable covenant which assured them life everlasting. Yes, the covenant was irrevocable, a Brother might "backslide" but in the end he would enter the kingdom. Once a child of God, always one, and it would be incongrous to contemplate one of God's children burning in Hell.

Thomas H., who still kept his residence at Fort Bend, came now and then and the old father was with him often. Thomas H. Borden had never given up the idea of a home in the Bend and a big plantation just over the river. His dream of Louisville was gone and the town of Richmond just below the Bend was assuming importance. The Thompson ferry was still operated although it was becoming obsolete for another one was operating below the Bend which was more in the line of traffic.

Just across the river a young doctor, Edward Long, with his young and beautiful wife and his forty Negro slaves had opened a plantation and they became welcome neighbors to the Tom

The Gail Bordens Go to Galveston

Bordens. Dr. Long was a semi-invalid and showed symptoms of lung trouble.

One evening a waggoner with a new vehicle drawn by a showy pair of horses and accompanied by a Negro handy man drove up the sandy road towards the Thompson ferry and the outfit stopped at Tom Bordens. The proprietor was an itinerant merchant, a dignified peddler with an assortment of goods and merchandise. He was a tall blond, straight as an Indian, and although he spoke with a brogue he was interesting and, a woman would be quick to say, attractive.

Swen M. Swenson, who was twenty-four, was a Swede who had landed from an immigrant ship at the mouth of the Brazos a few months before and had become attached to the mercantile house of Adriance at Columbia, and was extending their business by the enterprising method of taking the goods to the customer, and was visiting the scattered plantations which were multiplying year by year as slave-owners from the States came to Texas.

The young Swede and the Bordens were soon acquainted and when the itinerant merchant came, as he often did, he always visited with Tom Borden. Swenson became acquainted with the Dr. Edward Longs and was induced to give up his mercantile venture and become a farmer and take charge of the Long plantation. When Dr. Long died the next year the young Swede, after a seasonable time, married the beautiful and wealthy widow and for ten years lived the life of a Southern planter. Then came the broader life for which his character and talents fitted him and he moved from one enterprise to another until he became the founder or the head of one of the great banks in New York City and the founder of the great House of Swenson. Thirty years later he and Gail Borden often visited on lower Broadway and talked over the days when they were younger and the trials through which they had emerged and sometimes they met in their old age when they were making periodical trips back to Texas to enjoy the winter sunshine and revisit familiar scenes.

Swenson, like Gail Borden, was a Union sympathizer when Texas seceded. He was living in Austin at that time and had accumulated large land holdings and much money. The secessionists were making it very uncomfortable for those who refused to give aid and comfort to the Southern Confederacy and often such persons were hanged by officious committees who wanted to get rid of them and perhaps plunder their estates. Swenson was under surveillance by one of these committees and one night in 1861 he was scheduled to be hanged. Hearing of this by a friendly warning, he bestrode a mule and rode across the Rio Grande where he remained for three years.

The Gail Bordens Go to Galveston

There was a thriving business going on along the Rio Grande and in Matamoros conducted by Mexicans and refugee Texans who handled cotton hauled overland from Texas plantations and shipped out from Matamoros under foreign flags. Swenson, who was a mercantile genius, embarked in this trade during his enforced exile and prospered. From there he went to New Orleans at the close of the war where he continued his business and from there to New York.

When the clouds of war were gathering and Swenson saw danger ahead, he took forty thousand in gold and cached it in the chimney of his Austin home, carefully covering the treasure with masonry. After the war was over he came back and had the bricks removed and found the gold intact.

After the war Gail Borden had a treasure cached in his then extensive milk plants, as we shall see.

These pleasant Galveston days when Gail Borden's life was running smoothly, his days at work in the offices of the Galveston City Company, his leisure in his fig orchard laboratory, his children growing more interesting each year, his wife in the bloom of her womanhood, were halcyon and could not last.

The great specter which forever pointed its bony finger and shook its phantom hand at all dwellers in the Southland in those days, was the dread yellow fever. Time and again, always in the summer season, it made its visitations all the way from Charleston to Galveston, and always it abated when the frost fell. In the late summer of 1843 it made its periodical visit to the Gulf Coast and one fine day in the early autumn when the Island was in the full bloom of late summer, when the oleander with its various colors made each garden a blaze of glory and the trade-winds blew so soothingly, so softly that one must believe the world was immune from pestilence and death, the awful news swept the little seaport city that a man had died with yellow fever and that others were stricken with it. There was a panic—wagons, crowded carriages, people hurrying little children along in groups, Negroes with wheelbarrows bending under great burdens, crowds hastening to the wharves and crowding the boats that were frantically struggling to get to sea—to go somewhere, anywhere. All were fleeing from something silent, unseen, infernal. Those who were with the dead and dying and exposed often seemed immune, while others barricaded in their homes away from the victims, were seized upon and died—sometimes a whole family in a day.

This was sixty years before Walter Reid and his co-laborers, pioneers like Gail Borden, found the source of the infection in the harmless looking little yellow-backed mosquito

The Gail Bordens Go to Galveston

which flew unnoticed from house to house with his dregs of death. He was as common as the house fly and no one paid any attention to him.

The Bordens isolated themselves from contact with the dead and dying in a kind of quarantine, though kindly Gail went among them to offer aid from day to day. They watched every possible contact with infection except the unnoticed mosquito who flew in and out of the unscreened houses. Then when it seemed that the monster had been glutted with victims, young and old, gray haired men and beardless youth, little children who played in the shade of the liveoaks, Penelope, the still young beautiful wife of Gail Borden, for she was only thirty-two, sickened and died, followed a day later by their little daughter. The tall gaunt, kindly husband and father helped dig their graves and laid them to rest amidst the ever-blooming oleanders of their garden, within the sound of the murmuring surf which beats forever on the sandy shores of beautiful Galveston Island. Later he constructed a brick vault over their graves where they slept for forty years until removed to be re-interred with him when he had passed away.

Then came the north wind and the frost and the disease was gone as suddenly as it came.

Gail Borden told Reverend Baker that he was convinced that refrigeration was the cure for the malady and that he was going to build a

Gail Borden, Pioneer

huge refrigerator so that as soon as a person developed the first symptoms he could be kept in a freezing temperature until he recovered. He was half-way right but only half-way. But this forty years before the pioneer Pasteur discovered the germ theory of disease and sixty years before the pioneer Walter Reid discovered the culprit that carried the germ. Gail Borden's pioneering was along another but kindred line.

After the death of Penelope, Gail Borden looked more wistful than ever and walked in his garden and among his pots and pans and vats. He had developed an imperfect outline of a great idea, the concentration of meat juices and their preservation so as to make them food for the sailor on far seas, the traveler in desert places, the soldier on remote frontiers. He knew that much thought had been given to this enterprise and he also knew that up to now the expense of concentrating a beef creature into a few pounds had made the plan prohibitive.

At the very time he was patiently working with his crude apparatus, with no scientific training and with an imperfect knowledge of the scentific literature on the subject, another scientist, a member of the great philosophical societies of Europe, a "fellow" of high degrees, the great German chemist, the Baron Justus von Liebig, in his up-to-date laboratory at Geissen, was struggling with the same problem, though the Baron had never heard of Gail Borden and

The Gail Bordens Go to Galveston

probably did not know whether Galveston was in Texas or Timbuctoo. And it is doubtful if Borden had ever heard of Baron von Liebig, though he may have read of him up at Ashbel Smith's library at Evergreen, for the Baron was a man of much renown.

In those days (the middle 1840's) there was a very unusual person who lived in the coast country of Texas by the name of Ashbel Smith, the Honorable Ashbel Smith, Doctor Ashbel Smith, as he was variously called. His home was at Evergreen Plantation across the bay fifty miles from Galveston where he lived in barbaric bachelor quarters with his slaves and his hounds. A Connecticut Yankee by birth, his mother was an Adams. Graduated at Yale at nineteen he had gone to Carolina where he made a gesture at practicing law and did not like it. He went back to Yale and took the medical course and topped it off with three years in Europe, and on his return to America he heard of the Revolution in Texas and hurried thither, reaching the country a few weeks after the battle of San Jacinto. He was soon in local politics, and President Houston sent him as Envoy Extraordinary to the Court of St. James and since Texas could not afford a resident Minister at all the European Capitals, Dr. Smith was made Ex-Officio Envoy to Paris and such other places nearby where Texas required diplomatic services. Home from these missions he had been Secretary of

State in the Cabinet of two Texas Presidents and when the Republic had entered the Union he settled down at Evergreen where the skeleton derricks of the Goose Creek oil fields of today are a forest of gaunt towers.

Dr. Smith was a very small man with a thin straggly beard and great notions of his own dignity which his looks belied. He rode up and down the countryside on a vast rawboned horse followed by a pack of hounds which Governor Lubbock, a neighbor, always insisted never tackled anything more savage than a jack-rabbit.

But Dr. Smith was a scientist. He belonged to all the learned societies and was a contributing member of the American Association for the Promotion of Science. He had a library and kept up with the periodicals of this and other learned societies.

It was only a few hours sail across the bay from Evergreen to Galveston and he often dropped in on his friend Gail Borden, who spent all his hours free from the Galveston City Company in his handmade laboratory over which he had built rude sheds to keep off the sunshine and the rain and give him some privacy. And Gail Borden as often was up at Dr. Smith's plantation and deep in his literature.

All he could do with the calves he boiled down was to reduce them to a forbidding looking solid with the consistency of glue which in

The Gail Bordens Go to Galveston

the warm humid climate of Galveston Island would never become more than an unappetizing looking and bad smelling gelatine.

In the meantime the Baron von Liebig of Geissen had given up. He wrote, "From thirty-two pounds of lean beef free from bones and fat there is obtained one pound of true extract of flesh which from its high price cannot be an article of commerce." He therefore concluded that his "extractum carnis" would not become a commercial commodity and moved on to something else.

It was 1849. The Mexican war was just over and we had acquired half a continent which must be explored, and our explorers must cross vast cruel deserts. Exploring parties and emigrant trains who were fortunate enough to esscape the hostile Indians and parching deadly thirst, often starved to death. Then came across the western world the news of gold in California, and one hundred thousand people, men, women and children, forgetting the hostile Indians, the deadly thirst and hunger, were off across the Continent.

A party was starting from Galveston overland a thousand miles, and they talked with Gail Borden about food for their six months journey. He was through with this kind of pioneering in covered wagons, but was busy on another frontier. He decided to make them some glue extract, some "extractum carnis," and set up a large kettle and evaporating pan and reduced one hundred and twenty pounds of veal to ten pounds of extract of a consistence like melted glue and molasses. The weather was warm and rainy, it was the middle of July. He could not get the stuff to dry indoors or out of doors. At night after his friends had gone, and it seemed they had wasted one hundred and twenty pounds of good beef, the tired inventor sat staring disconsolately at the stinking mess he had made. Like Baron von Liebig, he might have concluded that this glue would never be made a commercial product. Then came an idea. Nearby stood a flour barrel and he half idly took a scoop of flour, mixed it with a portion of his glue, put it in the oven and baked it and left it overnight. The next morning he had a hard, well dried meat-loaf, and it was not only edible but palatable. This was his discovery, his first great invention. Here he had meat and bread in a combination which would dry and keep. They brought him six hundred pounds of beef and he soon had enough food in a single chest on one wagon to take his emigrant friends across the desert. He had combined Baron von Liebig's "extractum carnis" with bread and gave the world meat and bread in a durable concentrated form.

Chapter XI

GAIL BORDEN GOES TO LONDON

Gail Borden forthwith betook himself to Evergreen and told it to Dr. Smith and they pondered how to bring this great discovery to the attention of the scientific and commercial world. The next meeting of the American Association for the Promotion of Science would be at Charleston in March and Dr. Smith would attend. He had Gail Borden write him a letter telling of his experiments and his discovery, which he did with due formality, giving very much the detail which one would employ in an application for a patent. Dr. Smith transmitted the letter with one of his own to the President of the Association, who was a grandson of Benjamin Franklin, with learned comments and approval.

While this was being done Mr. Borden attended to the details of procuring a patent.

The American Association and the grandson of Dr. Franklin were duly impressed. The fame of the meat biscuit quickly spread locally and the little Texas papers told all about it. An Austin paper declared for it: "A man can now mount his horse with a month's rations in his saddle pockets and he needs no other cooking utensil than a tin cup."

Emigrants on the California trail, Texas Rangers on the long frontier, ships going out of Galveston, all sought the new commodity, and Gail Borden without accurately gauging this home demand, raked and scraped all his means together and built a factory to take the place of the cooking vat in the shed back of his fig orchard. On the site where the Gulf, Colorado and Santa Fé Railway station stands today he built a two-story brick building and installed a ten horse-power engine. To this he harnessed biscuit machines to knead and roll the dough, a mill to pulverize the biscuit, a "Savage" meat

Gail Borden Goes to London

chopper and cauldrons, in which he could boil seven thousand pounds of meat in a day. With two pounds of beef extract to three pounds of flour he had five pounds of food which defied the elements and withstood time and distance.

A circular was distributed telling all about the wonderful product, and a copy of it, probably the only one in existence, yellow with the age of eighty odd years, is in The University of Texas Library, bearing these incredible testimonials: The meat biscuit makes the finest known soup; reaches its highest perfection when boiled with vegetables; is irresistible in a pot pie; mixed with rice and sugar gives a superb pudding; is a perfect background for a mince pie, and may be used as a custard or any other desired dessert by merely varying the flavoring, etc.

John H. Brower of New York City, merchant, was induced to become agent and distributor in an effort to reach the shipping trade, and twenty tons of the product was made and shipped to New York. But it would require time to work up this trade, and the folks going on the California trail and the occasional ranger outfit and the few ships going out of Galveston did not furnish the volume of consumption necessary to take the seven thousand pounds of meat per day which he was feeding into the capacious cauldron. It was necessary to get a nation-wide, world-wide market.

Dr. Ashbel Smith came to the rescue with a

pertinent suggestion. The World's Exposition or the great World's Fair of 1851 was about to meet in London. Scientists from all the earth would be there, and the meat biscuit which had now been proven in Galveston and all Texas and talked about in the newspapers and scientific journals of the States should be presented there for an award of merit. Dr. Smith contemplated going to the Fair and Gail Borden should go with him.

So it was all arranged, the Governor of Texas was to appoint the Honorable Ashbel Smith delegate from or representative of the State of Texas and he would renew his old diplomatic friendships and meet the scientific brethren to whom he was more or less known. On the morning of March 7, 1851, a formidable document bearing the great seal of the State of Texas and signed by Governor Bell appointing Dr. Ashbel Smith delegate, was handed to Gail Borden for delivery to Dr. Smith, and he hastened to send it across the bay to Evergreen and to ask the Doctor to come down at once for a conference with him at the "factory."

A month later delegate Smith took the boat for New York, and Borden was to join him there as soon as he could finish up some business matters and they would go together to London. They walked together to the wharf on a windy March day—a tall, gaunt man and a brisk, bearded little fellow who scarcely reached the

Gail Borden Goes to London

tall man's shoulders. The short man wearing a high silk hat too high for him and a long black Prince Albert coat too long for him, waved good-bye from the deck of a New York-bound steamer, and the tall man hurried back to the factory to get things in order to follow on the next boat.

He had confidence in his new invention and he had boundless confidence in the Sage of Evergreen and was now ready to make the important step. He would resign from the Galveston City Company of which he had been executive secretary for twelve years. What was the petty salary to him now? Fame and fortune awaited him in the trade-world which must see the merit of his great invention. There were millions in it—Dr. Smith had told him so and would help him get the meat biscuit before the world and Russia and Turkey. The Directors of the Galveston City Company accepted Borden's resignation with regret and as a mark of esteem granted him a permanent wharf privilege near his factory site.

He gathered his scanty wardrobe and packed his chattels for the longest voyage in his life. He managed to find a high hat and a long black Prince Albert coat. All Southern gentlemen had these habiliments in those days, although they were often a trifle worn. All these details and many other petty matters, including plans for a long absence from his family, consumed more time than he had anticipated and he missed the first boat on which he had promised Dr. Smith he would sail and did not leave Galveston until April 8th. When he had finished all the details for his voyage and paid his bills, he had barely enough money to take him to London, but he trusted luck and the Lord and was off.

Dr. Smith was a prompt, punctual person and did not like being delayed, so he took passage for London as per schedule, leaving a long letter with ample instructions, bidding Borden to follow on the next boat.

When Borden got to New York and met the kindly agent-merchant Brower, he was well received and much encouraged. Brower was sure of success, so sure that he readily agreed to advance Borden money for the trip and authorized him to draw for more, if needed.

Again Borden missed the "next boat," the "Africa" which was sailing on April 23rd, but he managed to get two long letters on it to Dr. Smith telling him he was coming and telling him much of the kindness of Mr. Brower. In one of these he tells how he has weighed the matter of his going to London. Some of his friends advised against it, others in favor of it, but the deciding factor, he says, was the advice of Dr. Smith: "Your great experience and knowledge have acted on me like the pole star on the magnet and I will launch on the broad Atlantic on the next steamer." He does not fail

Gail Borden Goes to London

to add that he has taken the matter to the Lord in prayer.

He had read in the New York papers that the Emperor Nicholas of Russia was in London visiting the Fair and he suggests that Dr. Smith at once get in touch with the Czar of all the Russians and make contracts to sell him meat biscuit for all his people and all his armies. He had no thought that the late Envoy Extraordinary from the Republic to Europe at large would have any difficulty in perfecting this arrangement with the Czar.

Nor was the Sage of Evergreen idle while waiting for Gail Borden. He contacted the Committees of the great exposition and told them he was the advance agent of the now celebrated inventor of whom they had heard and presented samples of the meat biscuit with letters and testimonials as to its use, and the Committees went into a huddle and tested it and tasted it.

Then one day in May, Gail Borden wearing his high hat and his long coat landed in London and he and the Honorable Ashbel Smith were very busy for many days.

They repaired to the great Crystal Palace where the industrial, art, and scientific exhibits of the Fair were being displayed; 80,000 feet of space had been set aside for that young and vigorous nation, the United States of America. But the young, vigorous nation had done little to occupy the space and there were only two American exhibits. One was Cyrus McCormick's recently invented harvesting machine and the other was a small display of Gail Borden's meat biscuit with a legend telling something of its wonderful properties which Dr. Smith had arranged before Borden arrived. No other exhibits came and the American Consul at London managed to cover the bare space with an immense American flag. The merits of Borden's biscuit were duly presented to a scientific committee.

The "jury" of scientists to whom the matter was submitted heard a report from Professor Lyon Playfair and Dr. Edward Sally, who wrote, "No doubt exists as to the success of this experiment, as the starch remains unchanged and there is no evidence of putrification of the meat content." And the jury of which Dr. Smith was a member, found its verdict that the product was entitled to the highest award and then and there in the great Crystal Palace they bestowed on the good Gail Borden the Great Council medal—more than this they craved the privilege of presenting his name for honorary membership in the London Society of Arts which was accordingly so done, and the gentleman from Galveston was enrolled in the catalogue of the great.

Gail Borden's Galveston dreams now seemed fulfilled. Recognized by the scientific world as

Gail Borden Goes to London

the inventor of a product of staple diet which must be used to the ends of the earth, he was about to return home to enjoy the honor and emoluments that must be forth-coming. Full of assurance he and Dr. Smith sat down in their little London hotel one night in July, 1851 and divided up the world, the world that was waiting hungrily to feed on this new great food product. Dr. Smith was to have the world at large, outside the United States, in which he was to make contracts with any and all persons whomsoever, with any government, or governments, for the sale of the meat biscuit, and he was to secure patents, for all of which he was to have a stipulated percentage of all profits. A document evidencing these facts was duly signed and delivered to Dr. Smith in the office of the Legation of the United States in London. Two weeks later they seemed to think they had overlooked Russia and had some misgivings whether it was included in the former world-wide contract and so they made another in which Dr. Smith was given a special power of attorney to make necessary applications for a patent to the Emperor of Russia and was to have the same powers and privileges already granted as to the world at large.

These things done the gentlemen from Texas returned to New York where Borden at once plunged into the problems of handling the United States, and Dr. Smith, after a week, hastened home to wind up some petty affairs at Evergreen before starting on a world-wide tour.

Gail Borden was now fifty and with all the enthusiasm with which he and Thomas H. and John P. had plunged into journalism and surveying and real estate after the San Jacinto campaign, he landed in New York to begin his new commercial career.

Then, as now, one having a great idea to sell, a great industry to finance, must hasten to New York, that shrine of the money goddess. And then, as now, many were called and few were chosen by the fickle goddess of financial success.

All seemed fair and full of promise as long as Dr. Smith remained to encourage him, but after he had been gone a week the difficulties ahead became apparent, and on Monday morning, October 20th he wrote the Doctor: "Thank God, I have had another Sabbath's rest. If the weeks had eight days I would have given out. When you were here to cheer and encourage me it was not so difficult. All last week no sales, now $1600 in debt here, and I labor without rest. But I prayed to God all day Sunday and he came to my relief and today I feel as good as new."

All through the late autumn of 1851 Borden labored to get his product before the consuming public. His agent Brower had done his best to engage shipping interests with some

Gail Borden Goes to London

small success, and Borden began haunting the shipyards, hunting up Captains and owners of boats about to go on far voyages, interviewing stewards and sea-cooks, and giving them samples. Often the cook who had the last say would not like the looks or the smell of the biscuit, or if he tried to use it would not cook it right. And good Gail Borden would find himself early in the morning or late at night in the kitchen of some tramp schooner, cajoling a foreign sea-cook, and begging for the privilege of showing him how to prepare the meat biscuit so that it would not be sent from the table untasted, or thrown overboard, after the first taste. It had to be cooked just right, and few cooks knew how to do this, and fewer of them would take suggestions about it.

Then he tried the hospitals. While the cooks there were a little more approachable than those heathens he found on shipboard, yet the young Doctors whom he dealt with were impossible. They made fun of him as he came with his boxes and cans, and made fun of the soups which were made from the biscuit. Through a friend he got the attention of the head physician of Bellevue Hospital, and got the permission of the chief cook to go into the kitchen and prepare the food for ten patients that had been assigned him as a try-out. Into the kitchen he went, and while cooks and waiters stood about the tall, gaunt, tired man boiled and stewed and ladled out trial dishes for the ten patients, and trudged along to see them taste it. While nine of them said it was nice, yet the young Doctors "turned up their noses" and he went away discouraged.

All through the autumn he labored on and the day before Christmas he told his troubles to his "dear friend" Dr. Smith in a lonely letter: "My great concern is how can I raise money to sustain myself until sales begin . . . It is awfully cold here and I am tired of this northern climate."

His family was still in Galveston, and it was a doleful Christmas prospect. He told Dr. Smith in this Christmas Eve letter of plans to bring to the attention of the War and Navy Departments at Washington the great value of the meat biscuit on land and sea.

His good friend Brower, who was advancing him money to live on from week to week now counseled him to make vigorous effort to get the product adopted by the Army and Navy of the United States. Here would be a dependable market which would take the output not only of the little Galveston factory which his brother John was operating in his absence, but would justify a plant in or near New York. So with his usual earnestness and industry he turned to this undertaking. This seemed simple enough for he knew its merits and besides he had already contacted some of the army posts.

Gail Borden Goes to London

At this very time he had a letter from Colonel E. B. Sumner of the First Dragoons at far off Fort Leavenworth, Kansas, in which the Colonel had said to him: "I have tried the meat biscuit and find it all and more than the inventor thinks it is. To satisfy myself I have lived upon it entirely for several successive days and I am content that I could live upon it for months and retain my health and strength. In my judgment it is a very great discovery and must lead to important results. I am decidedly of the opinion that we ought to commence using it in the army at once and I believe from all active operations in the field the advantages of this food will be so apparent that it will become in general use in a few years."

He had similar letters from Sergeant Wright of the Eighth Military Department and from no no less a person than General Thomas Lawson, Surgeon-General of the United States Army.

The task assigned him therefore seemed easy, and he betook himself to Washington and began his efforts to have his products adopted as an army necessity.

Although Gail Borden had in his long active life encountered all kinds of people and almost every kind of obstacle, he had yet to learn something of that rare and perfect combination that existed in those days in Washington, between the government or army contractor and the Washington politician. All along the frontier and wherever army posts were located from San Antonio to the Canadian border and in the the Navy Yards as well, there were prosperous and opulent contractors who were furnishing beeves, beans, bread and other essentials for the use of the army and navy, and these contractors had their headquarters or their hindquarters in Washington where they had the necessary auxiliary of a political representation with whom they shared their profits.

All kinds of objections were made which hindered the adoption of the Borden product from month to month and from year to year, and all the while honest old Gail, bewildered at the delays, found himself going in a circle from one office to another and rapidly getting nowhere. In despair he went down to Washington and sought his old friend, United States Senator Sam Houston to whom he told his troubles. They sat on the veranda of the hotel one summer evening, and he went over the whole story with Senator Sam. Houston listened and turned to him slowly and said, "Gail, forty years ago I went up against this same game. I came here to Washington and called the attention of the Interior Department to the fact that contractors who were furnishing food and supplies on the Indian frontiers were charging exorbitant prices and making exorbitant profits; that they were sometimes in league with the army officials and I even went so far as to offer

Gail Borden Goes to London

to perform the same service at just about half the price. I had friends in Congress for I had been a member of Congress, and my friend Andrew Jackson was President of the United States. But these contractors and their political aides in and out of Congress jumped on me. A Congressman from down in Ohio denounced me on the floor of the House as an imposter and a fraud. I got nowhere."

"What did you do, Sam?" said Gail.

"Well, I took my cane, and right out in front of this hotel I walloped that Congressman within an inch of his life, and then I went back to the wilds of Arkansas and gave it up and from there I went to Texas."

* * * * * *

Though many British ships used the product sent out from the Galveston factory and Dr. Elisha Kent Kane, who departed the next year on his Arctic expedition outfitted with it, and although travelers continued to use it, all efforts to get it adopted as an army product were unavailing.

Dr. Smith had found much unfinished business down at Evergreen and had delayed his assault on the world markets and those of Russia.

Gail Borden wrote him many letters in which he told him his troubles. In one he wrote: "I am entirely out of money. You know I have borrowed large sums and all my property in Texas is held as security. I owe my father a large sum which is not secured. Won't you please see my creditors there in Texas and ask them not to push me, if they do my property will all tumble like a row of bricks."

In another he tells that he has talked with Mr. Dana, Editor of the New York *Sun*, and Horace Greeley of the *Tribune*, and they agreed that the government had treated him most rascally.

And in another: "Don't infer I have given up, for I know that my invention is one of the discoveries of the age . . . But the rub is, my debts are due. I have had to parcel out my family among my friends and relatives. My wife is in one place, my daughters in another and every piece of property I have is mortgaged. I labor fifteen hours a day. I am now keeping house— pay $18.50 per month rent with a room to work in and our living expenses are not more than one dollar per day."

These letters cover a period of more than four years, and the Doctor seems to have sympathized with him and encouraged him, and their friendship continued to the end.

In November, 1854 he wrote he was considering sending or taking a ton of his biscuit to Crimea for use in the hospitals, but he adds he is not only without means but fears his creditors to whom everything he has in the

Gail Borden Goes to London

world is mortgaged will not indulge him much longer.

In this November letter written three years after he returned from London he tells the Doctor—"I am greatly encouraged to embark in the milk business . . . This promises more sure results than the meat biscuit after these four years of effort."

In fact he had so far perfected his experiments made during these doleful years, 1851 to 1854, as to evolve his great idea and had already applied for a patent when he wrote this letter, but he had a three year struggle to get it granted.

In December, 1854 he was back in Galveston to look over the wreck of his fortunes as he put it, and he wrote the Doctor from there. "Thank Our Heavenly Father my health is good, my spirits unbroken . . . I set out to conquer or die and don't intend to cry over misfortune."

Although his patent for condensed milk had been pending more than a year and had been refused, he wrote in this letter that he was going to turn the meat biscuit enterprise over to someone else and would embark in the milk concentration business as soon as he could find persons who would advance the means. The failure of the enterprise in hand did not daunt him. Indeed as he wrote Dr. Smith his spirit was unbroken. He had at this period of his life evolved out of his religious fervor a philosophy or faith for the treatment of disease which he called the "Do nothing and hydropathic practice." He thought that by abjuring medicine, ample prayer and plenty of water, most any malady could be cured. A few weeks after he came to Galveston in December, 1854 he heard that his brother Paschal Pavalo was seriously ill at his Oyster Creek plantation up in Fort Bend and went at once to see him. After a week there he wrote Dr. Smith to whom he still confided almost everything, "I found him in the third stages of pneumonia, stuffed with drugs. I commenced my 'do nothing' practice and in twenty-four hours he was improving and now is convalescent. God be praised for his mercies."

On this trip to Texas he was trying to sell his scattered lands and he still owned a tract up near the Mormon Mills in Burnet County. He heard a rumor that grains of gold had been found in the lands on Sandy Creek, and he was in great need of this commodity and drove up to see if any of these manifestations were on his land.

He met an old friend there, Noah Smithwick, who had owned a blacksmith shop adjoining the Borden shop at San Felipe thirty years before, and Smithwick has left an interesting account of his visit. He says Borden confided to him the secret of his theory of medical treatment, or his "do nothing" system. "Nine times

Gail Borden Goes to London

out of ten," Borden told him, "sickness is caused by overeating, or eating the wrong kind of food. The patient gets mad if you tell him this, so I take a grain of calomel and divide it into infinite particles and mix it with harmless starch, and tell the sick man that it has calomel in it, which is true, and that he must not eat while taking the medicine. He abstains from food while he takes the harmless pill and gets well."

He returned to New York in March, 1855 and renewed his efforts to sell meat biscuit and get a patent on his process for condensing milk. Another year was to pass before he got past the Patent Office.

Chapter XII

NEW FRONTIERS

The Bordens were pioneers on wild frontiers. Norwich Township in Chenango County, Southwestern New York, where the four sons of Gail II were born early in the century, was an outpost of civilization where Indian tribes from nearby forests still came to trade with the settlers as the people were called. They followed the receding frontier lines south and south-

New Frontiers

west until they found the wildest and most dangerous of them all on the far coast of Texas. Here all four of the sons gave their best efforts for nearly twenty years to the reclamation of these wilds. And now at the middle of the century Texas had passed through the Colonial period, the era of the Republic and was a State in the Union with a line of forts and Federal soldiers all the way from the Rio Grande to upper Red River. The Bordens had helped move the frontier line west to the Pacific Ocean. They saw an orderly government and a prosperous people in the land they had helped reclaim, and the commerce of the world coming into and out of Galveston. Gail Borden had now turned his attention to a new and vaster frontier than had ever been sought by the pathfinder, the emigrant or the hunter—the great frontier of science where shadowy outlines still loom in obscurity after nearly another one hundred years have come and gone.

When the little Dutch janitor, who learned to grind glass and make lenses for a diversion, turned one of them on a drop of water and his horrified gaze beheld the monsters swimming in this particle of water lifted on a pin point, swimming, breeding, fighting and dying, he discovered a continent, a world if you please, vaster than the shores which lay before Columbus on his voyages one hundred years before. Hidden by ignorance, guarded by superstition, the realms of science lay beyond shadowy borders, obscuring those simple truths that then and now control the destiny of the race.

When Apert, the Frenchman, discovered the art of canning foodstuffs early in the Nineteenth Century, he crossed a frontier line into a vast realm full of infinite possibilities. Napoleon saw in it a means of feeding his soldiers while they carried on their work of destruction; the world has found in it the key to a storehouse with ample provisions to feed the race.

One of the next pioneers to cross this frontier line was Gail Borden, bending over his pots and pans and vats on Galveston Island, when he discovered that milk evaporated in Vacuo could be condensed without impurities. He did not know of germs, microbes and bacteria, for the great Pasteur, who was then approaching that frontier line, had not made the discovery which twenty years later startled the world and opened the pages to volumes of hidden truth which gave the human race a fighting chance to survive. Although Gail Borden did not know the names and habits of these creatures which Pasteur twenty years later saw and named, his intuition told him they were present, and he found a way to outwit them.

The world accepts these great discoveries of simple truth as a matter of course and accepts them with small gratitude to the pioneer who discovers them. It is all so simple, people say,

New Frontiers

anyone should have known it all the time. Few of the great inventions which have passed the Patent Office have escaped the challenge that they were so simple and fundamental that they lacked inventive genius, novelty—anyone could have thought of that. And in truth many of them were discovered by pure accident with as little ingenuity as one employs when he stumbles on a diamond in the rough, or gold in the waters of a mill-race. The world is ready to pirate and appropriate the work, the discovery, the invention, and such an attitude belittles the efforts of the discoverer.

A thousand volumes have been written and eagerly read about the so-called "great" Napoleon—

> *"That monster of a thousand thrones*
> *Who strewed the earth with hostile bones,*
> *And writ his evil deeds in gore,"*

while a dozen tell of the triumphs of the truly great Pasteur who saved a thousand times more lives than Napoleon sacrificed. The world worships its destroyers and often ignores its benefactors.

The wise saying has recently been attributed to Henry Ford, that "our truly great pioneering has not been in covered wagons but in laboratories and workshops."

There is a story told that the inspiration for the process which resulted in the perfection of

Borden's condensed milk came to Gail Borden while he was on his return from London in 1851. The story goes that cows were being carried shipboard to furnish milk for the children passengers. These cows sickened and died during the voyage and the result was that children sickened and died, and that the necessity for a pure milk product caused him to turn to that enterprise. It may or may not be so that he saw these things as he returned from London, but it is true that he had long ago discovered the idea and half-way evolved the process in his rude laboratory back of the fig orchard in Galveston. More than ten years before he had told Parson Baker who had seen him working with these pots and pans that he could and would condense not only meat but fruits, fruit juices, milks and other food products, condense them in such a way as to make them dependable and lasting food. The meat and bread combination in the meat biscuit which seemed to satisfy all man's food wants appealed to him as the greatest field of enterprise, but since this had failed in a commercial way he turned now to the idea of developing a dependable milk product. This was long before the days of refrigeration and the modern dairy. Here was a product that army contractors could not corner, a product which the dwellers in the fast growing cities of the country got with great difficulty, one that could not be transported any distance, one that in its natural state was subject to the most rapid deterioration. He reasoned all this and went to work. What he now set out to do, in fact what he had demonstrated to himself could be done, was to accomplish the preservation of milk by the simple removal of water accompanied by security against occurrence of possible detriment from the time the milk was drawn from the cow until the process was completed. The idea which occurred to him and which ultimately proved the merit of his invention, was that this evaporation should take place in a vacuum pan to prevent contamination.

He was aware that numerous attempts had been made to preserve and solidify milk as well as to find acceptable substitutes for it and he knew also that all had proven failures up to now. Scientific friends advised him that his aim in one respect was too high, that it would be impossible to retain all of the butter uninjured in connection with the other solid constituents of milk, that a removal of all or a part of the cream would be found to be necessary as a preliminary step. But he knew that if he accomplished nothing more than condensing skimmed milk he had accomplished little or nothing.

Thoroughly convinced that with the proper protection from injurious atmospheric influences during the process of evaporation he could eliminate the water and retain all of the fat, he proceeded to the completion of this idea.

But he found serious difficulties in an attempt to carry this method into practical operation. A very troublesome one was adhesion of the albuminous constituent of milk to the inner surface of the vacuum pan. The foaming of milk under lessened pressure involved the liability of certain loss by boiling over or being drawn out of the vacuum pan through the pump. An experienced sugar boiler observing his attempts, with hope to render assistance, pronounced the method utterly impractical for the evaporation of milk, and his persistence in trying to employ it, sheer folly.

During the years after his return from Europe and while he was still struggling with the financial problem of his meat biscuit and even before his optimistic nature permitted him to see its failure, he was at work further experimenting with milk. He was living a kind of hand-to-mouth existence in these days, and his resources were going lower all the time. Although he still considered Galveston his home he was all the time in the East in and out of New York and Washington.

He spent some months in a little village near New Lebanon, New York, where there was a Shaker Colony which had dairy herds, and he got together some apparatus and continued his experiments there. His most trouble was the deterioration of his product after complete evaporation. The evaporation and elimination of

New Frontiers

water was simple enough. It was not until 1853 that he had satisfied himself that the slightest exposure in the process of evaporation spoiled the product, and although neither he nor the scientific world knew of the germ menace, he must have then gravely suspected it, for he found after a hundred experiments that only milk evaporated in a vacuum pan could be depended on, hence he declared this idea his discovery, and it was.

The vacuum pan for evaporation had long been in use in the manufacture of sugar and fruit juices because it would allow evaporation at low temperatures and avoid the use of excessive heat which would burn and discolor the product. No one had conceived the idea that this vacuum process was essential to protection against unknown germs. Meats, sugar and fruits were not so easily contaminated as milk.

The learned Commissioner of Patents in Washington could not be convinced that the exclusion of air was essential to the purity of the condensed product and declined the patent. He thought milk freshly taken from the cow could be evaporated in the open air as well as in vacuo, and said so.

Then came another long year of further experiments and arguments with the Patent Office. Borden must prove this fact to others as he had proven it to himself and get their evidence for use in the Patent Office.

The Englishman, Grimwade, who had used a vacuum pan for condensing milk and had gotten a patent on specifications wide enough to include any method of evaporation, included one which specified the use of warm air, the air which Borden was sure should be excluded. Grimwade had missed the point.

Borden's name was now high in the scientific world, for the financial failure of his meat biscuit had not obscured the fact that he had made a great discovery, obvious to everybody but the army contractor and his political auxiliary in Washington.

He went to his friend Robert Macfarlane, the self-made Scotch scientist who since 1848 had edited the *Scientific American,* who well knew the tribulations of the amateur inventor. His discoveries in the art of dyeing had met just such obstacles, and he was sympathetic. He went with Borden to watch the experiments which would demonstrate that only the pure milk product could be gotten from the vacuum pan with all air excluded, and being convinced said so in his journal and gave his affidavit to that effect to be filed with the Commissioner of Patents.

All this took time and it took money, and Borden was flat broke. But he never lost courage, never complained to anyone but Dr. Smith to whom he poured out the contents of a weary heart. His hair which was graying at forty was

New Frontiers

much grayer and thinner at fifty-two, but he plodded on with his simple direct way.

Mr. John H. Currie, now head of the Belmont laboratories came to his aid and let him make experiments in the laboratory and gave the same kind of a testimonial which Robert Macfarlane had given. Armed with these evidences the inventor and his patent lawyers made a final assault on the Commissioner with the result that the patent was granted in August, 1856, three years and three months after the application was made. These, and five years after his return from London, had been long weary years.

In September, 1855, when all hope for the meat biscuit was about gone and after the Patent Office had twice denied him a patent on his milk process his fortunes were at their lowest ebb, and he wrote his last long letter to Dr. Smith closing a five year correspondence which gave an intimate glimpse into the character and soul of Gail Borden.

"After my return from Texas," he wrote, "I was very ill and adopted the 'do nothing treatment' and soon recovered." After recounting repeated failures and repulses in his efforts to sell meat biscuit he tells Dr. Smith that his friend Brower who has helped and encouraged him so many years has grown tired of him and shows great coldness.

"It has been weeks," he wrote, "since he has

said more to me than a formal good morning and this hardly audible. I owe him $2,000 and he wants it. I am at his place every day and am writing this letter from his desk. With no source of help but from him and with two children to support I assure you I employ a scale of economy which we never dreamed of in those days when we looked down the streets of London from St. James. You ask how Uncle Gail holds on. Well the answer is simple. The religion of Jesus Christ as set forth in the Gospel sustains me as it will anyone who puts his trust in it. I have my little son John, a pious child, and we read God's Holy word together and pray together. In this way I am sustained, my friend. You ask Uncle Gail what are you going to do. First, I am going to stick to the meat biscuit as long as I can make any sales. Second, I am still making progress in my invention of concentrating milk. I am happy to inform you that I have succeeded in concentrating milk 80% without the use of sugar and it is soluble in either hot or cold water. It is a beautiful article. I do not hesitate to tell you that should I live two years I shall present the world an invention of vast import. Milk will be as common on shipboard as sugar. Remember what Uncle Gail has told you. He will be the inventor of this great process."

This was written in September, 1855, four years after he returned from London, a year be-

New Frontiers

fore he finished his three year fight with the Patent Office and nearly three years before he got his first modest little milk plant going at Burrville.

For aid rendered him in three years contest with the Patent Office he had parted with three-eighths of his patent. He now had before him the still more difficult task of financing which he well knew from sad experience was a heartbreaking, hazardous venture. He soon parted with two-eighths more for the promise of financial assistance he never got.

While Borden was worrying with the Patent Office after his return from Texas in 1855 he met an urbane gentleman named Thomas Green, a lawyer and landed proprietor who had an estate near Washington, and who, interested in Borden's ideas, invited him to be his guest. For several months he enjoyed the hospitality of Mr. Green while he waited and argued with the Patent Commissioner and his examiners. Borden's means were now gone and he insisted on paying Mr. Green with work he did in odd hours, plotting his Virginia estates and advising him about land interests which the thrifty Mr. Green had acquired in Texas. He was working his way through the Patent Office and paying his board by doing chores. And the thrifty Mr. Green succeeded in getting an interest in Borden's patent. There were promises of money to build a plant and what not, which the genial host had implied rather than written in the dealings he had with Borden during this stormy winter.

On the strength of these promises Gail Borden was up in southern Connecticut early in 1856 seeking a location for his factory. All of the details for a building and machinery had been well worked out by him in his mathematical way.

Wolcottville, Litchfield County, Connecticut, was a wee village in 1856, beautifully set in the Naugatuck Valley. It had half a dozen houses, two inns and one church and a wealth of matchless scenery. It was at the site of Torrington of today. Here the tall, gaunt Yankee-looking Texan told the village folks of his plans to establish a factory in their midst which would furnish a market for their milk products, and he was received with open arms. There was no Chamber of Commerce to welcome, no Rotary Club to hear his ambitious plans, but he managed to get the heart of the village folks who could do no more than wish him well.

His chief aid and dependable ally in these Wolcottville days was old Darius Miner, owner and proprietor of the chief store in the village, oracle and ex officio head-man of the town. With the aid of Darius an old abandoned building which had been used as a carriage factory was located. He purchased this site and began to convert the defunct carriage factory into a

New Frontiers

modern milk condensery. But the urbane gentleman who had promised him aid and procured from him substantial interests in his patent would not even advance money to meet his payrolls for putting the old house in order. Destitute, he left Wolcottville and borrowed enough money from a friend in New York to return home to Galveston. The failure at Wolcottville seemed the deciding blow. It seemed that his condensed milk enterprise had gone the way of the meat biscuit. Although he did not know what he would do next, he nevertheless knew he would do something, for he never gave up. He prayed to his God.

When Gail Borden came back to Galveston in 1857 he was literally at the end of the row. He still had some scattered lands in Texas from which he got no revenue and for which he could get nothing and they were mortgaged. His brother Tom now lived in Galveston and was running a butcher shop. It is said that he rode from his house to his shop each day on a great white ox, a kind of advertisement of his bovine business. John P. was ranching down on the Nueces, and Paschal Pavalo, farming up in Fort Bend. It was a gloomy homecoming, and the abandoned meat biscuit factory stared at him to remind him of prior failure. He had not only failed to get finances for his milk factory, but had hopelessly involved his patent rights in contracts with his late promoters.

A week after he reached home he had a letter from one of his late backers and at his solicitation he returned to New York two months later. Some of the tangles were taken out of their complex dealings and he was promised money for another try-out. It was decided to abandon the Wolcottville carriage factory, and a still smaller village five miles north was selected this time.

The inducement for the change was a better water supply and an abandoned mill building somewhat more promising than the old carriage factory at Wolcottville. Then too all observers must agree that the millsite on the wooded hillside at Burrville with its waterfall and view of the valley below was more picturesque than the carriage factory site—although the scenery was not a moving motive.

Money was now promised and some of it was forthcoming, and pipes and cans and tanks and a miscellany of freight was unloaded at the little railway station at Burrville and hauled out to the millsite; Gail Borden, who was as ever his own chief mechanic and craftsman, was busy and happy hurrying his second venture to completion.

Just as it seemed assured the panic of 1857 struck the country and found its way to remote Burrville. The source of his funds was stopped. He could not pay his accumulated bills. He was sued for debt and the enterprise was stopped

New Frontiers

and again he seemed at the very end of his row.

Not knowing where to go or what to do he took the train for New York on a vain hunt for something or somebody and crowded his tall, wistful figure into a railway seat. It was one of those accidents which determine great issues in life, his chance meeting that day with Jeremiah Milbank, a passenger on the same train, an incident which was to mean much in the life not only of the Bordens but the Milbanks. Gail Borden had the rare faculty of Stephen F. Austin of telling his story with simple forceful directness, and with Borden, as with Austin, no one doubted his sincerity. In an hour, as the train rumbled on, Borden had interested and convinced Milbank, and money was advanced, the lawsuits were settled and the Burrville plant was completed.

In May, 1858 *Leslie's Weekly* carried an advertisement—"Borden's Condensed Milk prepared in Litchfield County, Connecticut, is the only milk ever concentrated without the admixture of sugar or some other substance and remaining soluble in water. It is simply fresh country milk from which the water has been evaporated."

Later experiences disclosed that the product was improved by adding sucrose or cane sugar, the purpose of this to inhibit the growth of bacteria and other organisms.

The Burrville plant was now operating and

Borden's Condensed Milk was ready for market —all that was needed was a market. The market meant the city folks who could not get fresh milk and meant New York, the nearest heavy center of population, and to New York they went. First they changed the name from Gail Borden & Company to New York Condensed Milk Company and for the next two years the Burrville factory was able to put out the product faster than the indifferent public would buy it.

It was a meager beginning. People did not know what condensed milk was and its many uses and advantages had to be demonstrated to them in a more or less inventive manner. Samples of the milk were first carried around from house to house in a handbag and gradually the people began to learn of the great value of the product and its many uses became known and the number of its regular customers began to grow. Then it was served from quart cans transported in a pushcart through the streets of the City of New York. That first Borden milk wagon was a crude and humble precursor of the thousands of fine, sturdily built horse-drawn and motor vehicles bearing the name Borden which may be seen on the streets of New York and Chicago and almost every other city in the United States today, distributing Borden's Milk Products.

Borden's Eagle Brand was now on the way

New Frontiers

and in less than two years it had been demonstrated that it was a success, but its progress was slow and there was little prospect of substantial financial returns in the near future.

Gail Borden, who now lived at Burrville and gave all his time to the enterprise, managed to squeeze out enough money over operating expenses for a living for himself and family, but little more. He was convinced now that Burrville, like Wolcottville, had been poorly selected and that his plant needed a location where there were more numerous dairy herds and a better dependable supply of fresh milk. With this in view he set out to explore. His friend Darius Miner, who knew the country far and near, furnished a horse and buggy, and one day in the fall of 1860 they started out to search the countryside.

Down in Dutchess County, New York, they stopped at the village of Wassaic at the narrowest part of the valley where the mountain ranges north and south seem to meet and the river runs between. Here was scenery, water and what more, a country far and near with ample herds. Gail and Darius went home convinced that this was the place.

But Banker Milbank was not convinced that an investment in a new plant was wise at this time. The one at Burrville had paid but small returns. The public was taking to the new product slowly and expansion seemed of doubtful wisdom in 1860. In fact it would have probably proven premature and entailed losses but for the unseen events which followed.

But Borden was impressed with the necessity of getting near a more dependable milk supply, in a denser dairying country, and perhaps the intuition which told him of germs and microbes long years before the world knew of them, told him that something unusual was ahead in 1860. Down at Wassaic he found one Noah Gridley who had means and who owned the property wanted for the new plant. He induced Noah to invest, and the plant was begun in the latter days of 1860, and the workmen were hammering away on it early in 1861.

The tall, gaunt, Yankee-looking promoter walked about the unfinished plant as the spring advanced and wondered if he was wise in making this extension, and if he would ever earn enough money out of the enterprise to pay his debts. Perhaps he prayed about it to the Lord, for as he had written Ashbel Smith nearly ten years before, he could not carry on but for his faith in prayer. But it was now ten years since he and Dr. Smith had left Galveston for London, and so far his prayers had met little response. They had been the cruelest ten years of his life, even more gloomy than those days a quarter of a century before when with his printing press on Eli Mercer's wagon he was fleeing at a speed of ten miles per day from Santa

New Frontiers

Anna's army. He was young then and had time to recover from his misadventures. But now it was different. He was sixty and poorer than he had ever been in his life. He walked the floor in these days.

In these early spring days of 1861 another tall, ungainly and very homely man was walking the floor. In March Abraham Lincoln, who had come out of the Indiana woods was inaugurated President of the United States. He was faced with problems—should he let the Southern States who had seceded go and see the Union dissolved—"Let the erring brothers depart in peace," as Horace Greeley advised. In April the secessionists fired on the flag at Fort Sumpter. In May, Abraham Lincoln issued his call for volunteers. In June, Gail Borden and Noah Gridley had finished the Wassaic plant. In October the Northern armies were on the march and the soldiers were carrying Borden's Eagle Brand in their knapsacks. It was the first time in the military history of the world that an army went to war carrying a dependable milk supply.

But for the war the progress of the Wassaic plant would have been little faster than the one at Burrville, and the introduction of Borden's milk products would have been slow. It would have succeeded maybe but only after a long tedious time. Probably another generation would have passed before the product would have been accepted, and Gail Borden would have been gone. The march of the armies meant a market for every ounce that could be produced. Army contractors with their political auxiliaries in Washington could not corner or handle the milk supply. Gail Borden's fortune was made. In every soldier's knapsack, in every camp and every hospital in the Northern armies, there were cans of Borden's Eagle Brand, and the Wassaic factory was running day and night.

In the long bloody war which followed these early Wassaic days Gail Borden remained in the North, for like his friend, Sam Houston, his sympathies were with the Union. His second son, John, was a soldier in the Northern army. But the Bordens down in Texas were of the South. Thomas H. Borden's oldest son, John Rolden, who was now nearly thirty, enlisted in the Southern army, and served until his death in 1864. The younger son, James Cochran, who was born at the Borden home in the Fort Settlement in 1835, raised a company and was in the Southern army until the end. John P. Borden's oldest son, Sidney Gail, though only nineteen when the war began, enlisted the first year. During the third year of the war the old father, Gail II, died at the age of eighty-six at the home of his son Thomas H. in Galveston. All during the years Gail III had signed his name Gail Borden, Jr. and he was nearly sixty-three when his father died and he dropped the

New Frontiers

"Jr.". Paschal, the third son of old Gail, died at his plantation home in Fort Bend in 1864.

The demand made by the war brought a wide expansion of the Borden industry and new units were built. A great plant was constructed at Brewster, New York, twenty miles south of Wassaic and fifty miles from New York City, and another of still greater proportions out at Elgin, Illinois.

For a number of years after the war Gail Borden, who had now dropped the "Jr." from his name, lived in Brewster in a spacious home built high on the main road and ornamented by a long double line of tall slender cedars through which one approached the portals of his Colonial mansion. When winter came he journeyed back to Texas sometimes going by boat to Galveston and as often by train and lived in the sunny hill country of Southwestern Texas amidst scenes familiar from long ago. Here he rode over leagues he had surveyed for Colonists forty years before and visited with his old comrades of other years.

At Brewster he was a civic leader, attended church in his open surrey and taught a Sunday school class and read the Bible with a feeling that amounted to eloquence.

After the death of Penelope in Galveston in 1843 he had married a widow, Mrs. Stearns, and upon her death a few years later he married

Mrs. Emaline Eunice Church, who was the wife of his later days.

The close of the war found Gail Borden a wealthy man and his name linked with a great enterprise. His two sons were now grown, men of promise. His daughter, Philadelphia Wheeler, was married and he had added to his family two lively sons of his last wife by first marriage.

Austin had been dead thirty years. Sam Houston had passed away two years before, and Gail Borden was now the most celebrated living Texan.

Chapter XIII

LAST YEARS OF GAIL BORDEN

The close of the war in 1865 saw the Borden milk industry firmly established and its products in general use throughout the country, and Gail Borden had made his fortune. While he remained President of the companies he gave less of his time to them each year. His sons Henry Lee and John were now men in their thirties and took an increasing interest in the Borden business.

His daughter, Philadelphia Wheeler, born in Galveston in 1837 and named for his mother, had married J. W. Johnson. In the early 1870's the Johnsons had taken up their residence in Columbus, Texas. Each year after the close of the war Gail Borden spent his winters in Texas. The presence of his daughter and her children in Texas led him to covet a residence near them. Then too he had never been reconciled with the utter failure of his meat biscuit enterprise years before. Since then other methods of preserving meat had made his biscuit obsolete.

In Southwest Texas at the close of the war there were vast herds of cattle that had accumulated in the land which had for countless ages been the winter grazing ground of the buffalo, that vast country between the lower Colorado and the Rio Grande. It was these immense wild herds which started the trail drivers in 1865 and for twenty-five years they were gathering and taking these herds up the trails which in 1870 reached all the way from below Bexar across Red River and Oklahoma to the railway lines that were being built west across Missouri, Kansas and Colorado and on to the Pacific. It is estimated that an average of three hundred and fifty thousand cattle were driven over these trails each year for over twenty years. Along the coast country these cattle were so common

Last Years of Gail Borden

and so cheap from 1865 to 1870 that processers built plants at the seaside where drovers would bring herds which would be slaughtered for their hides and tallow which were sent to market by sea.

Here, Gail Borden reasoned, was a chance to make another try-out of preserved meats.

At this time the Southern Pacific Railroad which terminated at Columbus, was being constructed on west to meet a construction coming from the west which soon made the southern transcontinental line from New Orleans to Los Angeles and the sea. One Thomas W. Pierce of Boston was President of the Southern Pacific, and his work-gangs were just west of the Colorado. He was a friend of Gail Borden with whom he talked much about Texas. President Pierce suggested to President Borden that there would be a market for meat products with these construction workers for several years—all these things led Gail Borden into his last business venture.

He and Milbank organized Borden's Meat Preserving Plant and began a factory at the then terminus of the railroad extension nine miles west of Columbus at a place he called Borden, and it still bears that name. His oldest son Henry Lee, took charge of the enterprise, a large tract of land was bought, and a meat packery to can roast beef was built.

On the hills of Harvey's Creek nearby, an

attractive site was chosen and he built homes for himself and his son, and his brother John, who was then past sixty, built a home just across the creek. Gail would spend four or five months of the year here and the remainder of the year in the North.

From here on April 22, 1872, he wrote his old friend Moses Austin Bryan, Stephen F. Austin's nephew, an interesting letter. "Your letter calls to mind very forcibly incidents of an olden time when the Texans vanquished Santa Anna, a time which tried men's souls. Although it was thirty-six years ago yesterday since the battle of San Jacinto was fought I can recall many thrilling scenes enacted during the years of 1835 and 1836. Although a sickly man at that date I am now in my seventy-first year, having already lived my three score and ten years. I thank the Giver of all good that my life has been so wonderfully preserved. I can hardly realize that you are a grandfather. I have a grandson, Gail Borden Johnson, thirteen years of age, who is now in Connecticut attending school. You perhaps may remember that during the late Civil War I had a son and daughter with me in the North, my oldest son and daughter remaining in Texas during the time. Since 1867 I have spent a large part of the winters in Texas in Bastrop County. I am now engaged in the construction of setting up meat preserving works on Harvey's Creek about nine

Last Years of Gail Borden

miles west of Columbus on the Henry Austin five league tract. The design of the establishment is to put roasted beef into cans and seal them up for market. Also to make an extract of beef to be put up in the same manner. It has already cost a large amount and is still far from completion. The company is corporate under the name of Borden Meat Preserving Company, the stock being owned by Mr. Milbank and myself. Mr. Milbank is my partner in the condensed milk business. I agree with you that Texas at least is one of the most desirable parts of the world to live in. Immigrants are coming, new settlements are forming, new life and energy even among the old Texans are noticeable. It would be highly gratifying to me, had I any leisure, to pay you a friendly visit and have a long talk about old friends long since deceased and of many others who still survive. It would be a social treat, a social feast and I should enjoy it very much. Bring your wife and others of your household and let us have a visit on Harvey's Creek at Bordenville. Brother John and perhaps Brother Tom would partake in the feast and would enjoy the meeting—what say you? Before closing this letter I must write the name *Stephen F. Austin,* my patron and my best friend. There is no man living or dead whose name and memory are cherished more by me."

He went back North this year and the next,

and in the autumn of 1873 he and his wife and his grandson Gail Borden Johnson landed in Galveston on their way to Borden and he stopped for a visit with his brother Tom. Just then news came that there was yellow fever at Columbus and he tarried quite a while at Galveston. His grandniece, Willie B. Borden, daughter of James Cochran, granddaughter of his brother Tom, was then about the same age of his grandson Gail Borden Johnson and she had the traditional beauty and vivacity of the Borden women. Ten years later she and her second cousin, Gail Borden Johnson, were married.

Borden had aged perceptibly since his visit a year before and was a little more stooped. Here with Tom and family and a host of friends he celebrated his seventy-second birthday. A remnant of his old friends was there to welcome him, with the acclaim that is always present for the man who has succeeded. Dr. Ashbel Smith, self-opinionated and sprightly as ever, came down from Evergreen and they laughed about the time they divided up the meat biscuit world.

After a month in these familiar scenes so full of memories, memories that held faces long vanished, he went on to his home on Harvey Creek. There on the 11th of the following January, 1874, the old frontiersman passed away, and the great white soul of Gail Borden went back to the God who gave it. He did not

Last Years of Gail Borden

live to see the failure of his last enterprise. Beyond the market which the construction gangs offered there were few sales. The great meat packeries which had begun at Chicago nine years before were more practical and efficient. Besides, the railway rates which were requisite to get the product into the markets, were prohibitive. The Borden plant was soon abandoned, and for several years a warehouse full of unsold canned meats remained to tell of the failure of Gail Borden's last enterprise.

His son Henry Lee went back North and succeeded his father as President of the Borden companies.

Gail Borden's remains were taken to Woodlawn Cemetery, New York City, for burial and later those of Penelope, his first wife, were removed from Galveston and reinterred beside him.

His brother Tom survived him four years and died in Galveston in 1877. John, the youngest brother, lived nearly twenty years longer at his home on Harvey's Creek.

Ashbel Smith of Evergreen passed on in 1886.

They were a remarkable family, these four sons of old Gail II, and their lives are part of the history of the great Southwest, and a wonderful man was Ashbel Smith.

It is a common saying that successful men

are those who believe in themselves and who have confidence in their ability to succeed. Gail Borden believed in God. He was only the humble instrumentality through which the Great Spirit might work its wondrous ways if he by prayer and right living could keep in tune with the Infinite. The test of a man is his ability to take punishment, to breast reverses. It requires little courage to carry on when winds are fair and success crowns one's efforts. But he who can rise from failure after failure and go on with renewed effort is truly great. Measured by this test Gail Borden meets all the requirements for the great of human greatness. On that September day in 1855 when he wrote his last letter to Ashbel Smith he was standing by the wreck of an enterprise on which he had staked his all, but with a boyish buoyancy he confided to Dr. Smith that he was about to present the world with a great invention which would be a boon to the race. He had prayed to God about it, he and his little son John at their cheap lodging where they were living on one dollar per day.

Dull, heavy years of weary efforts and repeated failures followed this dreary day but he never faltered. And when he died on a day in January, 1874 out in the beautiful Colorado hills, he ended a career of usefulness and had been a benefactor to the human race. He left an unsullied name, and his life is an open book in which the world may read the story of a spotless man.

Among the pathfinders of the race, the pioneers of the ages, Gail Borden's name must be enrolled. He was a nobleman for,

> *"How e'er it be it seems to me*
> *'Tis only noble to be good.*
> *Kind hearts are more than coronets*
> *And simple faith than Norman blood."*

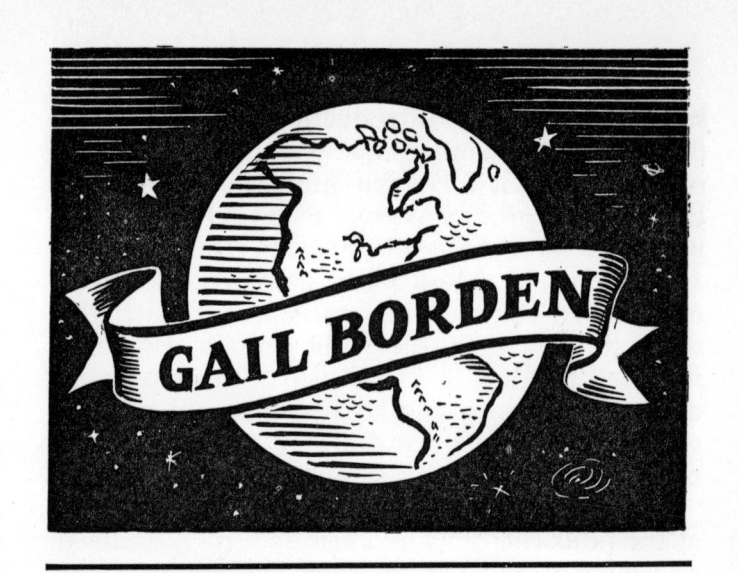

CHAPTER XIV

GAIL BORDEN'S NAME GOES MARCHING ON

Sixty-seven years have passed since Gail Borden died. The pioneers in the world of science have gone far and have wrought many changes, but the basic fact he discovered still lies at the foundation of one of the world's greatest industries. Mr. Otto Frederick Hunziker in his late work on condensed milk and milk powder

Gail Borden's Name

says: "Since the introduction of the process of milk condensing was invented and patented by Gail Borden numerous modifications of the process as well as entirely different processes have been invented in this country and abroad ... Most of the new processes have not proved commercially satisfactory with the result that the principle of the process originally invented by Borden and which consists of condensing milk in vacuo to a semi-liquid fluid is still used in the great bulk of the condensed milk produced in this country and abroad."

The completion of the Wassaic plant almost at the hour the Northern armies were mobilized and what it and the Brewster and Elgin plants did to supply these armies was something new in the world's military and industrial history. A young war correspondent of the New York *Tribune* named Charles A. Page, who was with the armies and in the hospitals and saw the value of this product, was sent to Switzerland as United States Consul at Zurich just after the close of the war. He conceived the thought of carrying the Gail Borden idea to that great dairyland and sent for his three brothers and they organized and operated the Anglo Swiss Condensed Milk Company which made a great success in Europe and finally brought branches of its business to this country.

A Swiss named Meyenberg, who worked in their factory, was years later the organizer of the Helvetia Company in the United States.

The condensed milk industry rapidly grew until long before the close of the last century, it was a gigantic business not only in this country, but also in Canada, in all the European countries, in New Zealand and Australia. In 1932 more than two and one-half billion pounds of these products were distributed in this country. At the present time the people of the United States consume more than twice as much evaporated milk as cheese and as much of it as they do ice cream.

According to figures in the United States Department of Agriculture the use of concentrated milks is increasing rapidly in this country even more so than all other forms of milk. It is probable that the milk supply of the future will comprise a greater and greater quantity of these condensed milks not only because of their public health advantages but also for economic reasons. Condensed milk not only provides a convenient supply, easy to store and conserve and transport, but also makes possible the utilization of surplus milk when over-abundant.

These facts give a faint notion of the great economic import of what Gail Borden first saw and did in his fig orchard laboratory so long ago.

BIBLIOGRAPHY

BIBLIOGRAPHY

The lives of the Bordens between 1822 and 1836 can only be told by a recitation of the leading historical events of that period. From the time that Tom Borden came with the Three Hundred until the Reconstruction which followed the Revolution and the Battle of San Jacinto in which the two younger brothers fought, the four Bordens were actors in the great drama which led to the formation of the Republic. They were a part of every forward movement during these years. The first nine chapters of this biography traces them through this eventful period.

Many, if not most, of the personal details are taken from old letters and diaries covering a long, wide range of years and from traditions gathered from members of the numerous Borden families.

While Gail Borden was a voluminous letter writer, none of the letters to him has been preserved. Many letters from him have been found here and there. His letters to Dr. Ashbel

Smith referred to extensively in Chapter XI, which well disclose Gail Borden's beautiful character are found among Dr. Smith's papers in the Library of the University of Texas. Letters from him are found in the Thomas J. Chambers Papers, in the Bryan Papers and many half forgotten files.

In 1850 a pamphlet was published by Gibson, printer, in Galveston which contained correspondence which passed between him and Dr. Smith with reference to Borden's meat biscuit. In 1872 Goodale, Secretary of the Maine Board of Agriculture, published a brief sketch of Gail Borden telling the world of his great accomplishments. I have copies of these sketches.

During the forty years I have been making historical research I have encountered and preserved from sources too numerous to mention, items with reference to Gail Borden with the thought that one day I would write his biography. During many of his early years in Texas there were no newspapers. During most of the time the few papers which were published gave little current matter of historic interest, and the written history of that period is largely confined to public documents, private letters and an occasional diary.

While I was engaged upon this manuscript a member of the Lapham family living in Iowa, wrote Gail Borden, Jr. of the Chicago *Times*, that he had a volume of letters that had passed

Bibliography

between the Bordens and Moses Lapham, 1828-1836. Through Mr. Borden I procured copies of this extensive file and they were very helpful.

In 1842-43 a young Presbyterian minister by the name of Baker was a pastor in Galveston and intimate with the Bordens. Some time later he wrote and published an account of his two years in Galveston which gave many of the interesting details which are found in Chapter X. As far as I know there is only one copy of this interesting book in existence.

—*C. R. Wharton*

Houston, Texas
February 28, 1941

INDEX

INDEX

Adams de Onis treaty, 18
Adriance, House of, 149
"Africa," the, 164
Alamo, the, 80, 98-99, 100-102, 108, 113
Almonte, Colonel, 106
Alarcon, Governor, 98
Allen, Ethan, 115
Allen, Captain John M., 138, 142
Allens, the, of Houston, 126-127
Alsberry, Horatio, 68
American Association for the Promotion of Science, 156, 159-160
Amite County, Mississippi, 29-30, 57
Anahuac, 71, 72, 80
Andrews, William, 49
Anglo-Swiss Condensed Milk Company, 211
Apaches, 99
Apert, 180
Arroyo Hondo, 14
Austin, Henry, 205
Austin, Moses, 19, 20, 37, 54
Austin, Stephen F., 12, 19, 22-24, 32, 34-51, 65, 72, 75, 76, 78, 81, 83, 84, 86, 87, 89, 91, 93, 124, 130-131, 132, 137, 193, 200, 204, 205

Baker & Borden, 69, 107
Baker, Don Jose, 69, 87, 103, 104, 107, 109
Baker, Captain Mosely, 100-102, 111
Baker, Reverend, 153, 182, 217
Baltimore, 10
Baptists, 59, 60, 144-148
Bastrop, Baron de, 44-45, 47, 48, 50
Bastrop County, 204
Bates, General, 142
Beard, James, 35
Bell, Governor, 162
Bell, James H., 38
Bell plantation, the, 129
Bellevue Hospital, 169
Belmont laboratories, 187
Bernard, the, 43
Berry, Radford, 79
Bexar stormed, 90-91, 96
Blackburn, Ephraim, 16-17
Borden and Company, Gail, milk dealers, 194
Borden and Company, surveyors, 126, 135
Borden, Gail, Jr.: birth, 2; migration to Indiana, 2-3; early schooling, 7; youthful appearance, 7-8; beginning of friendship with Stephen F. Austin, 22; invited to Mis-

sissippi, 24; life in Deep South, 29-30; marriage, 58-59; purchase of slave, 59; arrival in Texas, 60; birth of daughter, Mary, 61; on Austin's staff of surveyors, 61; starts in newspaper business, 69; in conservative element, 72; helps write first Texas constitution, 73-75; in charge of Austin's office, 75; makes map of Texas, 76, 130; Austin's admonition to, 78; relies on Austin's judgment, 81; to San Felipe, 84, 91; member Committee of Five, 86-87; stays with press, 102; letter to Burnet, 103; puts out Alamo edition, 107-108; family members, 115-116; returns to Fort Settlement, 119; becomes land agent, 120-121; reissues Telegraph and Register, 122; upholds Austin's honor, 125-126; engages in surveying City of Houston, 126-127; makes map of Texas, 130; indexes records, 131; on his honesty, 132; appointed Collector of Port at Galveston, 134; moves to Galveston, 137; controversy with Republic, 139-140; his faith, 140, 144, 168, 188, 196, 208; beginning of his inventions, 141-143; baptism of, 146-147; as Union sympathizer, 150, 198; life in Galveston, 151; death of wife Penelope, 153; ideas on yellow fever, 153-154; invention of meat biscuit, 156-158; encouraged by Dr. Smith, 156; in London, 159-167; resigns from Galveston City Company, 163; honored by scientists for meat biscuit invention, 166; begins commercial career in New York, 168; tries to interest sailors and hospitals, 169; struggle with War and Navy departments, 170-173; letters to Dr. Smith, 168, 173-176, 187-188, 215; meat biscuit enterprise fails, 175; theory of medical treatment, 176-177; embarks on milk concentration, 175; struggles for patent, 177, 181, 185-189; discovers principles of milk evaporation, 180-185, 210-211; his courage, 186-187, 208; works for Thomas Green, 189-190; others get interests in his patent, 189; proposes factory at Wolcottville, Conn., 190; failure at Wolcottville, 191; returns to Galveston, 191; moves to Burrville, 192; gets backing from Milbank, 193; Borden Milk Company begins, 194; moves factory to Wassaic, N. Y., 196; effect of Civil War on Borden enterprises, 197-199, 211; death of father, 198; constructs another plant at Brewster, N. Y., and third at Elgin, Ill., 199; marriage to Mrs. Stearns, 199; marriage to Mrs. Emaline Eunice Church, 200; most celebrated living Texan, 200; his fortune made, 201; winters in Texas, 202-206; tries again at meat preserving enterprise, 203-207; letter to Moses Austin Bryan, 204-205; development of condensed milk business, 212; pamphlets on, 216

Index

Borden, Gail (present Jr.), 216
Borden, Gail, Sr. (father), 2-8, 60, 61, 198-199, 207
Borden, Henry Lee, 115, 201, 207
Borden, James Cochran, 198, 206
Borden, John, 188, 201, 208
Borden, John Petit, 3, 61, 68-69, 79, 80, 81, 84, 88-89, 91, 100, 111, 118, 120, 121, 131-132, 134, 168, 191, 198, 205
Borden, John Rolden, 198
Borden, Mary, 61, 115
Borden, Morton Quinn, 115-116
Borden, Paschal Pavalo, 2, 7, 61, 62, 79, 80, 89, 91, 100, 111, 118, 119, 121, 134, 176, 191, 199
Borden, Penelope Mercer, 59-61, 115, 143, 148, 153, 154, 199, 207
Borden, Philadelphia Wheeler, 200, 202
Borden, Sidney Gail, 198
Borden, Thomas Henry, 3, 7, 23, 25, 26, 32, 36, 42-44, 46-50, 53, 56, 61, 62, 65-68, 69, 91, 102-103, 106, 108, 115-116, 119-122, 126-129; 134, 137, 148, 168, 191, 198, 205-207, 215
Borden-Thompson quarrel, 65-68
Borden, Willie B., 206
Borden's Condensed Milk, 193-194
Borden's Eagle Brand, 194, 197, 198
Borden's Meat Preserving Company, 203, 205
Bordentown, 127-128
Bordenville, 205
Bowie, James, 68

Bradburn, Colonel John Davis, 71-72
Brazoria, 69, 75, 81, 84, 85
Brazos, the, 33, 35, 42-43, 71, 73, 97, 102, 109, 110, 115, 116, 118, 121, 122, 126, 127
Brewster, N. Y., 199, 211
Brower, John H., 161, 164, 170
Bryan, Moses Austin, 204
Buffalo Bayou, 103, 115, 126, 130, 134
Burnet County, 176
Burnet President, 103-104, 107, 108, 116-117, 120, 121, 124
Burrville, Conn., 189, 192-195, 197
Bustamante, President, 77
Byron, Lord, 138-139

Cain, a Morton slave, 106
Calder, Robert J., 117
California gold rush, 157, 160
Caney Creek, 85, 86
Castleman, Sylvanus, 44-45
Catholics in Texas, 54-55
Charles IV, of Spain, 14-15
Cherokee Indian reservation, 74
Chicago, 207
Chicago Times, 216
Chihuahua, Mexico, 15-16
Chrisman, Horatio, 46
Church, Mrs. Emaline Eunice, 200
Cincinnati, 2, 122-123
Civil War's effect on Borden enterprises, 197-199, 204
Clay, Nestor, 74
Clay, Henry, 74
Clopper's Bar, 133
Coahuila and Texas, 63, 72, 78, 84-85, 93, 125
Cochran, James, 67
Collinsworth, Captain James, 87-89

Colorado, the, 42-43, 61, 72, 100, 102, 104, 115, 202
Columbia, Texas, 53, 75, 123, 126, 128-129, 130, 133, 149
Columbus, 179, 203, 205, 206
Comanches, 99, 134-135
Committee of Five, 86
Condensed milk: discovery by Gail Borden of principles of evaporation of, 180-185; Borden milk company begins, 196; in Civil War, 197-199, 211; principles of milk evaporation, 210-211; consumption of condensed milk products, 211-212; and *see* under Borden products and Gail Borden, Jr.
Congress of the Republic, 126, 128, 129-130
Congress, U. S., 173
Consultation, the, 84, 87, 91, 92, 99
Convention of 1832, 72-73
Convention of 1833, 73-75
Convention of March 2nd, 99, 122
Copano, 85, 97
Cos, General Martin Perfecto, 85-87, 89, 91, 112
Court of St. James, 155
Crimea, 174
Crystal Palace, 165-166
Cummings, James, 44
Currie, John H., 187

Dana, Editor of New York Sun, 174
Davis, Jefferson, 28-29
Davis, Samuel, 27-30
Decree of 1835, Mexican, 95
Dimmitt, Phil, 68
"Dutch janitor," the little, 179
Dutchess County, New York, 195

Egypt, Texas, 60-61, 104, 115
Elgin, Ilinois, 199, 211
Erwin, Dr., 67
Evergreen plantation, 155-156, 159, 162, 163, 165, 173, 206, 207

Fannin, Colonel James W., 84-86, 97, 99, 100, 113
Farias, Gomez, 77
Fifth Congress, 80
Filibusters, 18, 20
Filisola, 109, 118, 121
Fitzgerald, David, 35
Ford, Henry, 181
Forks of the Road, 110-111
Fort Bend *or* Fort Settlement, 34-35, 65, 66, 102, 105-107, 118, 119, 123, 148, 176, 191, 199
Fort Leavenworth, Kansas, 171
Fort Sumpter, 197
Franklin, Dr. . . . , 160
Franklin, Benjamin, 160
Franklin, Benjamin C., 117
French and Indian War, 14

Gaines, General, 110, 114-115
Galveston, 60, 70, 80, 103, 108-109, 115-119, 127, 129, 134, 137-141, 145, 147, 157, 164, 170, 173, 175, 179, 180, 182, 184, 191, 199, 206, 207, 216, 217
Galveston Bay, 36, 53, 70
Galveston City Company, 139, 151, 156, 163
Geissen, Germany, 154, 157
General Land Office, 80, 131-132, 134
Gibson, printer, 216
Godoy, 16
Goliad, 19, 87-88, 97, 124, 143
Gonzales, 86, 87, 89, 100-101, 109

Index

Goodale, Secretary of Maine Board of Agriculture, 216
Greeley, Horace, 174, 197
Green, Thomas, 189
"Green Valley," Miss., 30, 58
Gridley, Noah, 196-197
Grimwade, 186
Groce, Jared E., 24, 109
Guadalupe, the, 51, 100-101, 113, 121, 136
Guerrero, President, 77
Gulf, Colorado and Santa Fe R. R., 160

Hanks, Dennis, 6
Hardin County, Kentucky, 29
Harrisburg, 80, 103-105, 107, 110-111, 116, 123, 126, 133
Harvey's Creek, 203-207
Hitchcock, Lt. Ethan Allen, 115
Housing, pioneer, 5-6
Houston, city of, 126-128, 130, 133, 134
Houston, Sam, 55, 74, 92-93, 97, 100, 105, 109-112, 115-117, 119, 126, 131, 132, 134, 137, 155, 172-173, 198, 200
Huckins, Rev. James, 145-147
Hunziker, Otto Frederick, 210

Illinois, 1
Indiana, 1, 3, 5, 60
Ingram, Ira, 23-24, 46, 51
Ingram, Seth, 23-24
Interior Department, 172
Iturbide, Colonel, 38-39, 76

Jackson, President Andrew, 74, 110, 115, 173
Jefferson County, Indiana, 4
Johnson, . . . , colonist, 43, 46, 48
Johnson, Francis White, 79, 85, 97, 99-101

Johnson, Gail Borden, 204, 206
Johnson, J. W., 202
Jones, Randal, 49, 65, 66

Kane, Dr. Elisha Kent, 173
Karankawa Indians, 50
Kentucky, 3, 5
Knight and White Labor No. 6, 50, 65, 66
Knight, James, 48-49

Lapham family, 216-217
Lapham, Moses, 53, 55, 56, 62, 64-66, 68, 100-101, 111-112, 118, 126-127, 129, 134-135, 217
Lattimore, Dr. William, 24, 30-31
Lavaca, the, 53
Lawson, General Thomas, 171
Leslie's Weekly, 193
Liberty, Miss., 30, 59, 60
Liebig, Baron Justus von, 154-155, 157, 158
Lincoln, Abraham, 5, 28-29, 197
Lincoln, Thomas, 5, 27-29
Litchfield County, Conn., 190, 193
Little, William, 23, 35, 43, 49, 65
"Lively," the, 26, 33
London, 162, 165, 175, 182
London Society of Arts, 166
Long, Dr. Edward, 148-149
Long, Mrs. Edward, 148-150
Louisiana, 11
Louisville, Ky., 10
Louisville, Texas, 65, 68, 127, 129, 148
Lubbock, Governor, 156
Lynchburg ferry, 111, 112, 118, 133

Macfarlane, Robert, 186-187
Macon, Georgia, 59

225

Madison, Indiana, 4
Martin, Captain Wiley, 105-106
Martinez, Antonio, Gov., 19, 37
Matagorda, 85, 86
Matagorda Bay, 51
Matamoros, 97, 99
Matrimony in Texas, 55-56
McCormick, the Widow, 114
McGruder, Mr. . . . , 103
McKinney and Williams, bondsmen, 140
Mechanicsburg, 62
Medina River, battle of, 18
Mercer, Eli, 59-61, 73, 104, 107, 111, 196
Mercer, Rev. Jesse, 58-59, 145-146
Mercer, Silas, 58-59, 148
Mercer, Rev. Thomas, 59, 146
Mercer University, 59
Mexia, General Jose, 139
Mexico, 12, 17, 72, 75-77, 85, 86
Mexico, City of, 36-42, 93
Mexican Congress petitioned, 39-42
Mexican Constitution of 1824, 76, 88, 92
Meyenberg, 211-212
Milam Colony, the, 136
Milbank, Jeremiah, 193, 203, 205
Milk. *See* Condensed Milk
Miner, Darius, 190, 195
Minute Men, 87-88
Mississippi, 11, 51; life in, 26-27; River, 33
Mississippi Valley, Chambers, 10
Missolonghi, 139
Monclova, 78, 80
Monterrey, 19, 37, 38
Moore, Admiral, 138
Morgan's Point, 116
Mormon Mills, 176

Morton, William, 35, 48-49, 65, 106
Muldoon, Father, 56

Nacogdoches, 17, 19, 54, 71, 74, 79, 110, 130, 131
Nacogdoches-San Antonio Road, 128
Napoleon, 14, 180-181
Nashville, Tennessee, 122
Natchitoches, 12, 14, 33, 60
Naugatuck Valley, 190
Navidad, the, 75
Navy of the Republic, the, 138-139
New England, emigration from, 1-5
New Lebanon, N. Y., 184
New Orleans, 10, 12, 20, 27, 31, 32, 49, 60, 75, 118, 119, 121, 126, 139, 151
New Year's Creek Colony, 33
New York, 2, 150-151, 161, 164, 167, 168, 170, 184, 191-195, 207
New York Condensed Milk Company, 194
New York Sun, the, 174
New York Tribune, the, 174, 211
Nicholas, Emperor of Russia, 165
Nolan, Philip, 15-18, 36
Norwich Township, Chenango County, N. Y., 2, 178
Nueces, the, 128, 130, 191

Ohio, 1, 3, 65
Ohio River, the, 2, 5, 10-11, 31
Old Spanish Trail, 33
Old Three Hundred, 31-56, 49, 215
O'Reilly, Count, 12, 14, 15

Index

Oxford, Ohio, 62
Oyster Creek, 142, 176

Page, Charles A., 211
Palm Sunday massacre, 101
Panic of 1857, 192
"Parker" of Kentucky, story of, 63-64
Parma, Duke of, 14
Pasteur, 180-181
Patent Office, 177, 181, 185-187, 189
Peace Party, the, 83-84
Peach Point, 81
Pedraza, President, 77
Peebles, Dr., 79, 131
Piedras, Colonel, 71-72
Pierce, Thomas W., 203
Pigeon Creek country, the, 5
Pioneer home life pictured, 5-7
Plan of Igula, the, 38-39
Plantation life in South, 11; Protestants in Texas, 54-55 22-30
Playfair, Professor Lyon, 166
Pollock, Oliver, 12
Posey farm, 5
Protestants in Texas, 54-55

Red Lands, the 110
Red River, the, 33, 179, 202
Reid, Walter, 152, 154
Rhode Island, 2, 58
Richardson House, 12, 22, 24
Richmond, Texas, 48, 127, 148
Richmond, Virginia, 147
Rio Grande, the, 71, 73, 91, 94, 118, 150, 151, 179, 202
River travel and trade, 8-12
Robbin's ferry, 110
Royall, Richard Royster, 86, 91
Rusk, General, 117, 120
Russia, 163, 165, 173

Sabine, the, 51, 110, 113, 114, 128
Sally, Dr. Edward, 166
Saltillo, 77-78, 94, 96
San Antonio, 19, 34, 54, 55, 68, 73, 85, 86, 89, 97, 98, 134, 172; founding of, 98-99; River, 88, 98
Sandy Creek, 176
San Felipe Convention. *See* Convention of 1832.
San Felipe de Austin, 47, 62, 63, 65, 67, 69, 79-81, 84-87, 89, 91, 100, 102-105, 107, 110-111, 123, 130, 131, 133, 176
San Ildefonso, treaty of, 15
San Jacinto, battle of, 107, 111-112, 113, 204, 215; aftermath of, 114-115, 118; news of, 116-117
San Jacinto Bay, 46, 53
San Luis Pass, 115
Santa Anna, 72, 76-77, 81, 83, 85, 94, 96, 98-99, 102, 105-112, 116, 124-125, 204
Scientific American, the, 186
Sennecherib (reference to), 114
Sesma, General, 101, 109
Shaker Colony, 184
Smith, Dr. Ashbel, 155-156, 159-168, 170, 173-176, 186-187, 196, 206-208, 215, 216
Smith, Deaf, 68, 112
Smith, Henry, Governor, 97-98
Smithwick, Noah, 64, 176
Southern Pacific R. R., 203
Stafford, Martha, 119
Stafford, William, 118-119
Stearns, Mrs., 199
Sumner, Colonel E. B., 171
Swenson, Swen M., 149-151

Texas: opened to colonizers, 12; controversy over, by France,

Spain, 13-14; three hundred home seekers to come, 20; offering of land, 20: wild stories on, 21-22; see "Old Three Hundred"; lands allotted colonists, 40, 45-47; settlements, 1824 to 1832, 51; varied reports on, 52-55; land grant "bargains," 78-80, 125; war starts, 83; army, description of, 89-90; volunteer soldiers come to, 95, 97; declaration of independence, 100; refugees flee before Santa Anna, 102; war, 103-112; refugee families, 113-121; indebtedness of, 121, 126; constitution of Republic published, 122; Republic's first Congress, 123-124; election of Houston, 126; Congress meets, 126; selection of temporary capital, 128; land grants, 130; Land Office created, 131; capital moved, 132-133; navy, 138-139; cattle in, 202-203

Texas Rangers, 160

Texas Telegraph and Register, 69, 87, 91, 94, 103-105, 107, 122-123, 125, 126, 130, 133, 137

Thompson, Hiram, 67

Thompson, Jesse, 23, 49-50, 64, 65-68, 129

Thompson, Jesse, Jr., 67

Thompson's ferry, 105-106, 109, 148, 149

Tomson, Nancy, 59

Torrington, Conn. See Wolcottville.

Travis, Colonel William B., 80, 85, 98

Trinity, the, 46, 110, 113, 115

Turkey, 163

Turner, Colonel Amasa, 137

Ugartechea, Colonel Domingo de, 71-72

Urrea, General, 99, 101, 109, 116, 118, 121

University of Texas library, 161, 216

Velasco, 103, 121, 125, 133

Vera Cruz, 125

Victoria, . . . , 76

Victoria, Texas, 88

Viesca, Governor Augustine, 78

Villa San Fernando de Bexar, 98

Vince's bridge, 112

Virginia Point, 117

Walker, . . . , colonist, 36, 43, 46, 48

War and Navy Departments, 170-173

War of 1812, 2

War Party, the, 83-84

Washington, city of, 115, 170-173, 184, 189, 198

Washington on the Brazos, 99, 100, 103, 110

Wassaic, New York, 195-199, 211

West Point, 17, 85

Wharton County, Texas, 60

Wharton, William H., 74-75, 78

Wheeler, Philadelphia, 2

White, Walter C., 48-49

Whitesides, Uncle Jimmie, 63-64

Wilkinson County, Miss., 30

Williams, Roger, 2, 58, 82, 148

Williams, Samuel M., 79, 125, 130

Index

Wolcottville, Litchfield County, Conn., 190-192, 195
Woodward, Demis (Mrs. T. H. Borden), 56, 116, 129
World's Fair of 1851, 162, 165
Wright, Sergeant, 171

Yellow fever plague, 151-154, 206
"Yellowstone," the, 133

Zurich, Switzerland, 211

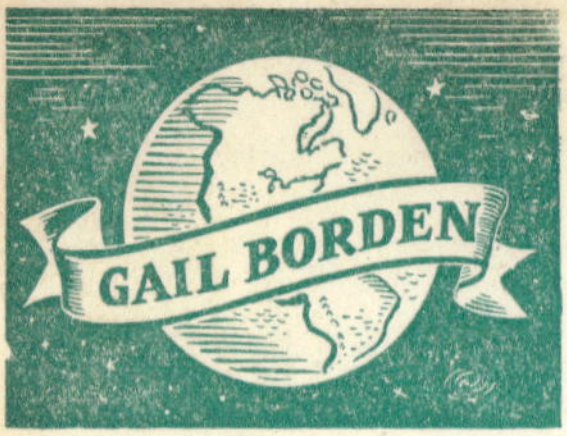
GAIL BORDEN

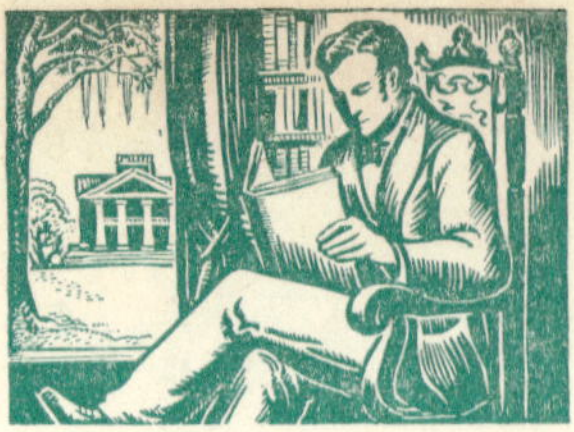

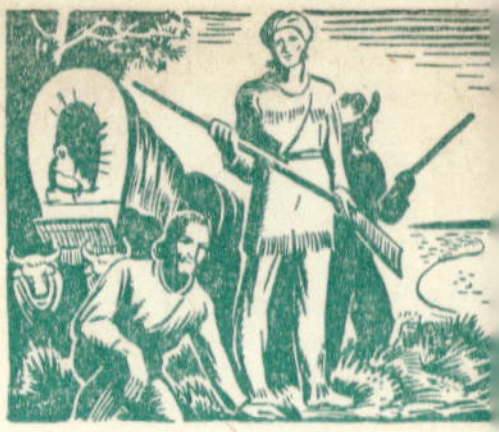

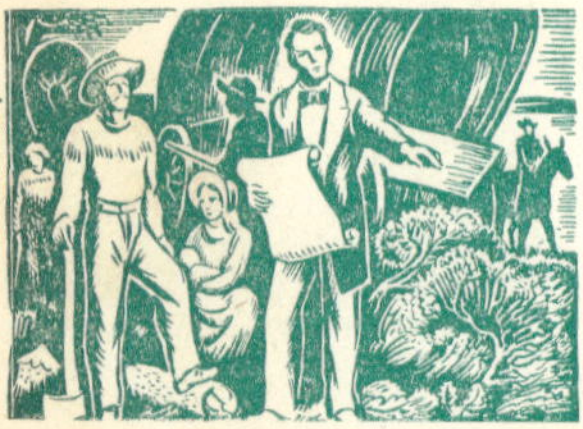

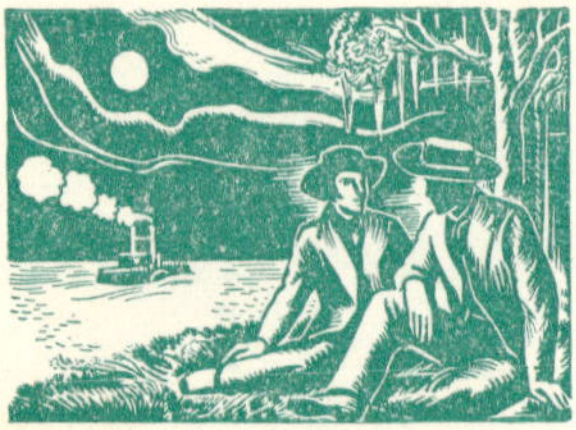

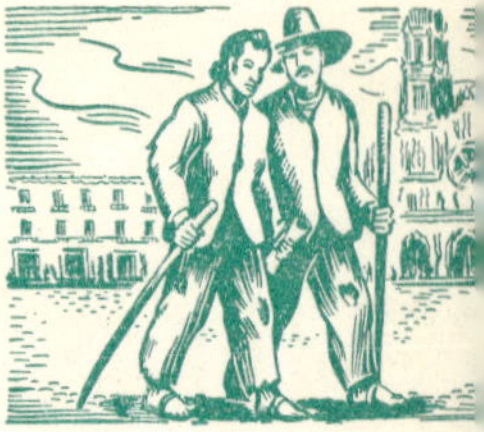

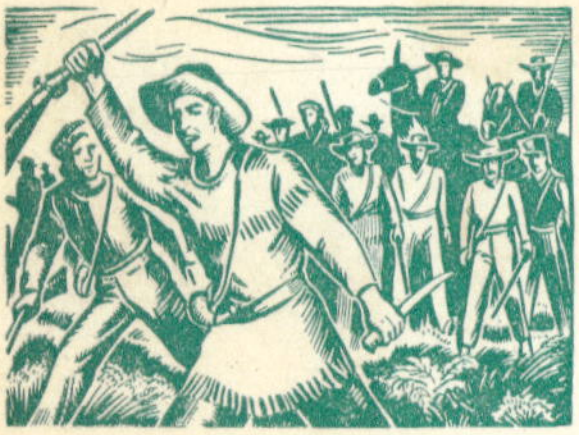

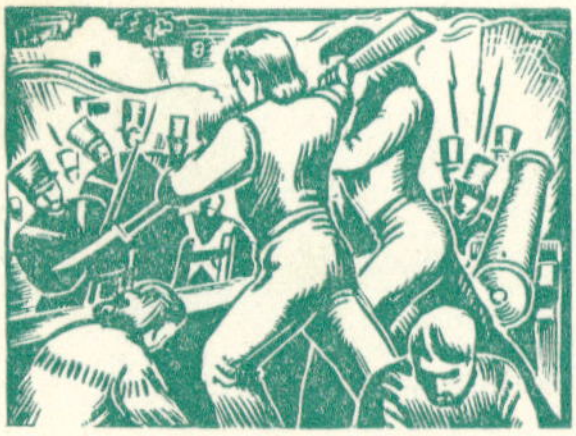

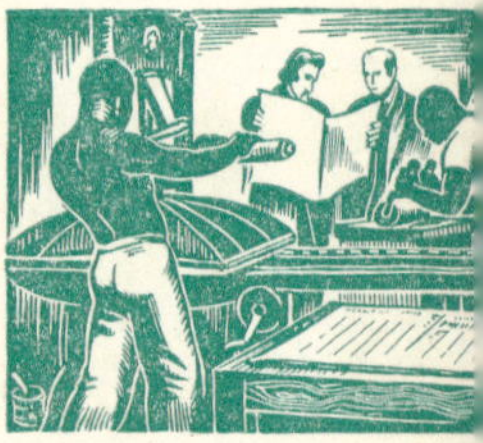

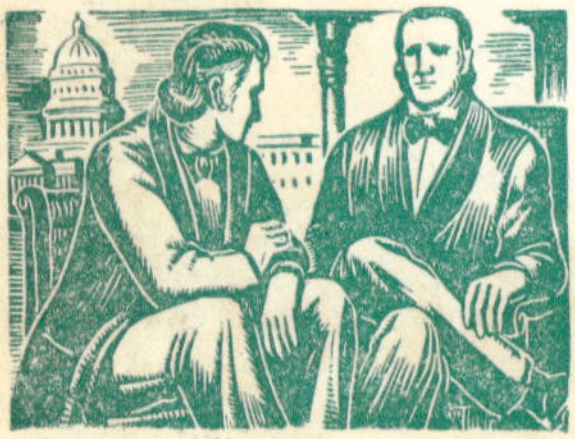

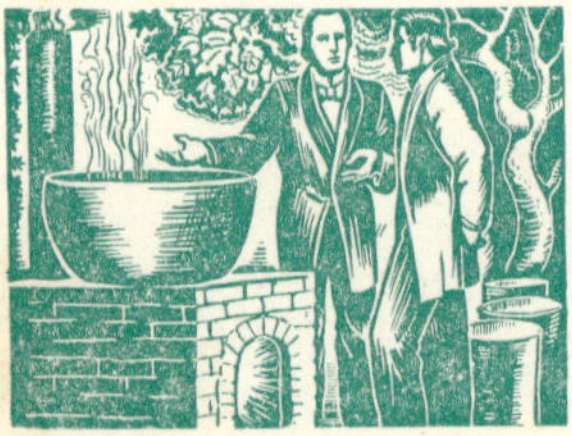

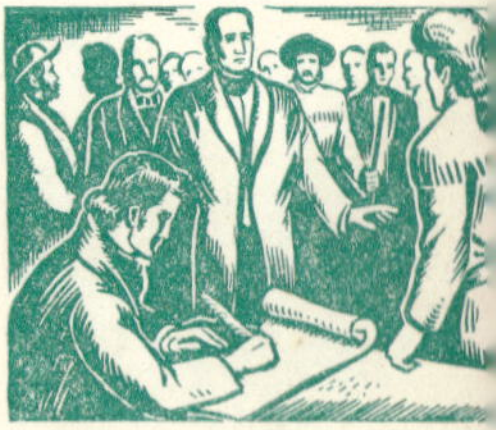

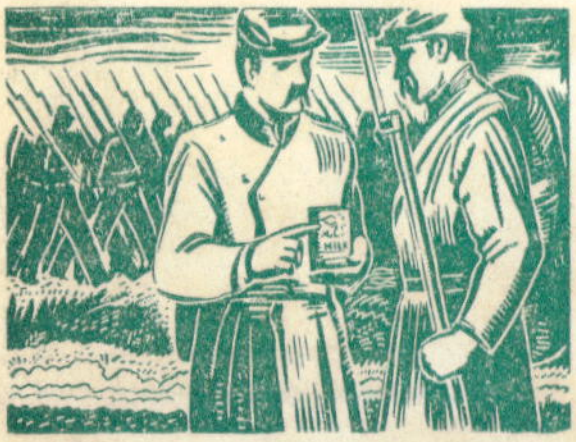

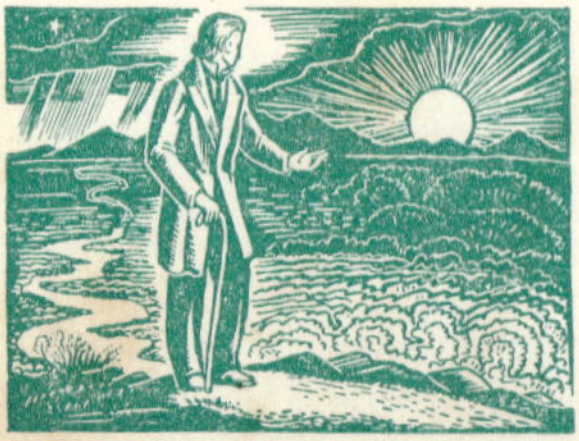

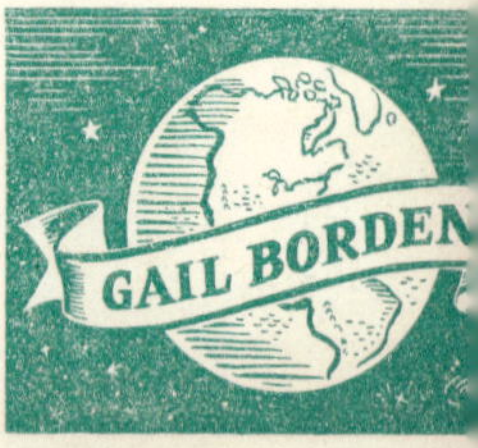
GAIL BORDEN